WALKING IN MENORCA

$

About the Author

Paddy Dillon is a prolific walker and guidebook writer, with nearly 60 books to his name and contributions to 25 other books. He has written extensively for many different outdoor publications and has appeared on radio and television.

Paddy uses a palmtop computer to write his route descriptions while walking. His descriptions are therefore precise, having been written at the very point at which the reader uses them.

Paddy is an indefatigable long-distance walker who has walked all of Britain's National Trails and several major European trails. He lives on the fringes of the English Lake District and has walked, and written about walking, in every county throughout the British Isles. He has led guided walking holidays and has walked throughout Europe, as well as in Nepal, Tibet, and the Rocky Mountains of Canada and the US. Paddy is a member of the Outdoor Writers and Photographers Guild.

Other Cicerone guides by the author

WALKING IN MENORCA

by

Paddy Dillon

2 POLICE SQUARE, MILNTHORPE, CUMBRIA LA7 7PY
www.cicerone.co.uk

© Paddy Dillon 2013
First edition 2013
ISBN: 978 1 85284 688 6

Printed by KHL Printing, Singapore
A catalogue record for this book is available from the British Library.
All photographs are by the author unless otherwise stated.

Base for route maps © Editorial Alpina, SL

Emergencies

If emergency assistance is required on land, phone 112 and explain the nature of the incident to an English-speaking operator. If a rescue is required, a response might be mounted by the fire service (bombers) or the police. The police can be contacted directly, phoning 092 for the Policía Municipal, 091 for the Policía Nacional or 062 for the Guardia Civil. Alternatively, for a medical emergency, phone 061. For sea rescues, phone 112 or 900-202202.

Advice to Readers

While every effort is made by our authors to ensure the accuracy of guidebooks as they go to print, changes can occur during the lifetime of an edition. If we know of any, there will be an Updates tab on this book's page on the Cicerone website (www.cicerone.co.uk), so please check before planning your trip. We also advise that you check information about such things as transport, accommodation and shops locally. Even rights of way can be altered over time. We are always grateful for information about any discrepancies between a guidebook and the facts on the ground, sent by email to info@cicerone.co.uk or by post to Cicerone, 2 Police Square, Milnthorpe LA7 7PY, United Kingdom.

Front cover: The sandy beach of Platges de Son Bou on the south coast of Menorca (Camí de Cavalls, Stages 2 and 3)

CONTENTS

Map Key

main route		church or hermitage/cemetery/cross
alternative route		archaeological site
start point/finish point		ruined castle/watchtower
start/finish point		bunker/stone cattle pen
alternative start/finish point		stream/gorge
dual carriageway		lake
main road		marshland
local road		water source/well or drinking trough
paved track		cave
dirt track		hotel
footpath		restaurant
high-tension line		museum
town boundary		information centre
limit of protected area		tourist office
parking area		hospital
village centre		viewpoint
building/ruin		point of interest
lighthouse/telecoms mast		bus stop
		picnic site
forest		
brushwood and meadow		
farmland/rock		

N

0   1 mile

0   1km

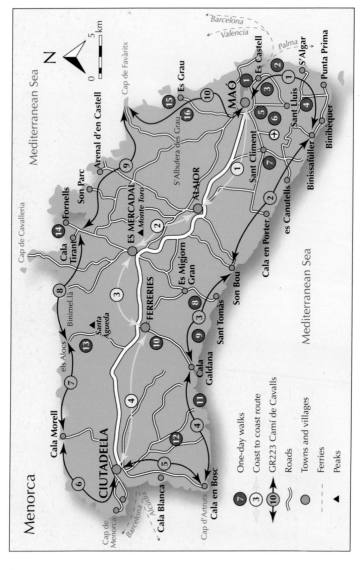

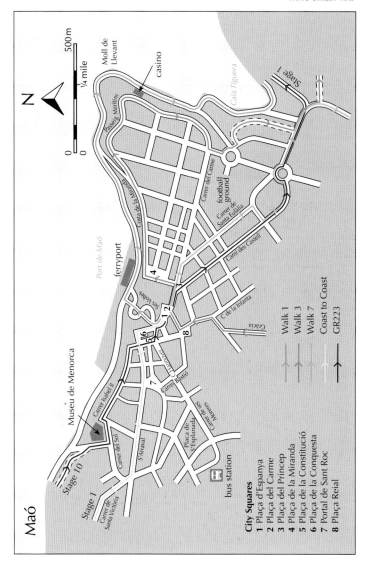

Maó

City Squares
1 Plaça d'Espanya
2 Plaça del Carme
3 Plaça del Príncep
4 Plaça de la Miranda
5 Plaça de la Constitució
6 Plaça de la Conquesta
7 Portal de Sant Roc
8 Plaça Reial

Walk 1
Walk 3
Walk 7
Coast to Coast
GR223

9

A track heads inland through dense woods at Alzina de Dalt (Walk 13)

INTRODUCTION

Looking towards Cap de Fornells (Walk 14)

The Mediterranean island of Menorca was a British possession for the best part of the 18th century, and it remains a firm favourite holiday destination for British visitors today. Sunshine and sandy beaches were considered a sufficient draw during the 20th century; however, since the year 2000, trail-blazing initiatives have led to the creation of a scenic long-distance trail right around the island and a network of interesting walking and cycling routes across it.

Outdoor enthusiasts are rediscovering Menorca, quartering the island in search of rugged cliff scenery, splendid beaches, amazing archaeology and fascinating historical sites. Routes pass through dense woodlands and cross steep-sided valleys, but never venture too far from useful facilities. The island has abundant accommodation, a good bus network and plenty of places offering food and drink along the trails.

This guidebook explores Menorca by means of 16 one-day walks, spread all over the island, and one four-stage walk across the island, together totalling almost 260km (160 miles). The long-distance GR223, or Camí de Cavalls, is also included, and measures an additional 185km (115 miles). It completely encircles the island, and takes about ten days to complete. In short, there is enough to keep a keen walker occupied for a whole month!

covered in small hills, dissected by a network of steep-sided valleys, or *barrancs*.

LOCATION

Menorca is one of the three Balearic Islands, basking in the Mediterranean Sea between southern Spain and northern Algeria. It is located from 3° 44' W to 4° 17' W and 39° 47' N to 40° 06' N. Its name is derived from the fact that its size is 'minor' (*menor*), when compared to Mallorca, measuring only one-fifth the size of its larger neighbour. At 695km² (268 square miles), Menorca is only slightly larger than the Isle of Man. The highest point on the island rises only to 362m (1188ft) on Monte Toro. While some maps suggest that Menorca is almost flat, in reality most of the island is

GEOLOGY

Menorca has many rock types, but the most important distinction is between the north and south of the island. Northern Menorca (Tramuntana) features the oldest and most convoluted rocks: approximately 400 million-year-old Devonian strata. These beds are chiefly exposed between the central and northernmost point of Menorca, and also along the east coast.

Rocks from the Triassic, Jurassic and Cretaceous periods – 300 to 65 million years ago – flank the older beds throughout the north. The rock types are complex, but red sandstone and grey slate are common. These

The spiral-striped lighthouse on the rugged Cap de Favàritx lies just off the GR223 route

break down to form golden sandy beaches and grey pebbly beaches respectively. The northern hills are remote, rugged and densely forested, although many valleys and plains have now been cleared for agriculture.

The southern half of Menorca (Migjorn) is a gently sloping limestone plateau, riven by a succession of steep *barrancs*. The rock was formed in a shallow sea in the Miocene period, approximately 25 million years ago. Where the limestone reaches the coast, it generally forms sheer cliffs and rock-walled coves, often with blindingly white sandy beaches at their head. This limestone provided the building material for the vast bulk of the island's archaeological sites.

Areas of dense woodland are separated by rugged fields criss-crossed with drystone walls. The southern half of Menorca is more accessible than the north, and is where most of the resorts are to be found.

HISTORY

There are over a thousand ancient monuments dotted around Menorca, to say nothing of more recent historical structures. The island has been settled for thousands of years, as well as being attacked and colonised by almost every neighbouring Mediterranean power. The most absorbing ancient sites are talaiotic settlements, dominated by stone towers, or *talaiots*, and T-shaped *taulas*. Later periods are notable for the construction of fortifications, especially around the coast. The table below lists the key events.

One of the two Navetes de Rafal Rubi, which can be reached by a short detour from the first stage of the Coast to Coast walk

4000BC	Neolithic hunters also herd goats on Menorca.
2300BC	Bronze Age people build navetas to bury their dead.
1400BC	Stone talaiot towers are built, along with T-shaped taulas.
900BC	Phoenician traders establish links with Menorca.
800BC	Greeks supplant Phoenicians and dominate trade.
650BC	Carthaginians supplant Greeks and settle in Menorca.
123BC	Romans, led by Metellus, completely conquer Menorca.
404AD	The islands become the Roman province of Balearica.
425AD	Vandals exert their influence over the islands.
534AD	Menorca comes under Byzantine control.
707AD	The first of many Moorish raids on the islands.
859AD	Vikings raid the islands, but the Moors remain dominant.
903AD	The islands become part of Moorish Al-Andalus.
1085	The islands become a Moorish Emirate.
1114	First of a series of Christian raids on the islands.
1232	Jaume I assumes control of Menorca without conquering it.
1276	Jaume II inherits the Balearic Islands from his father.
1287	Alfonso invades Menorca and remaining Moors are evicted.
1311	Sancho rules Mallorca and Menorca, which both flourish.
1349	The plague reaches Menorca from mainland Europe.
1350	Under Aragonese control, the islands' fortunes suffer.
1479	The kingdoms of Aragon and Castile are united.
1492	America is discovered; the islands decline further.
1535	Barbarossa lays siege to Maó and enslaves many inhabitants.
1558	Pirali raids Ciutadella and enslaves most of the inhabitants.
1571	Turkish ships are destroyed, bringing an end to Turkish raids.
1652	The plague once again ravages Menorca.
1708	The British invade Menorca and meet little resistance.
1722	Island governance is transferred from Ciutadella to Port Mahon (Maó).
1756	The British are expelled by French forces.

1763	The British regain Menorca in exchange for other islands.
1782	The British are expelled by the Spanish.
1798	The British again invade and recapture Menorca.
1802	Menorca is ceded to Spain under the Treaty of Amiens.
1836	Religious institutions throughout Spain are suppressed.
1936	Spanish Civil War, in which Menorca supports the Republicans.
1939	Menorca surrenders last in the war, through British intervention.
1960s and 70s	Menorca's tourist infrastructure develops.
1978	Spain's new constitution establishes Balearic autonomy.
1983	The Catalan language is restored to everyday use in Menorca.
1986	Spain joins the European Union.
1991	Laws are passed protecting nearly half of the island.
1993	Menorca is declared a World Biosphere Reserve.
1995	Parc Natural de s'Albufera des Grau is established.
1999	Reserva Marina del Nord de Menorca is established.
2000	Legislation is enacted to restore the Camí de Cavalls.
2002	Spain switches from pesetas to the Euro.
2010	The Camí de Cavalls is fully waymarked and opened.

The attractive, narrow, rocky inlet of Cala Alcalfar and the village of Alcalfar (Walk 2)

A large car park surrounded by farmland at Alfurí de Dalt (Walk 13)

LANDSCAPE

The underlying geology and thousands of years of human influence have shaped the landscape of Menorca. Seen from the air, the island is compact and almost entirely surrounded by cliffs, broken by occasional sandy or pebbly beaches. Inland a patchwork of fields is criss-crossed by drystone walls, and there are also extensive forests, small woodlands and areas of rugged scrub. In places the underlying rock is exposed where vegetation struggles to cover it. Many areas are arid, but there are a few lagoons that attract a variety of birds.

By contrast, some fields are remarkably lush and green, ideal for grazing black and white Friesian dairy cows and native red cows. Some of the valleys, or *barrancs*, that slice deep into the landscape carry running water, but many are dry. Most of the countryside features houses and farms, some of them old, stone-built and ornate. Some areas are dotted with curious *barracas*, or circular stone-built cattle-sheds, with a stepped profile reminiscent of ziggurats.

The island appears almost flat in some places, but there are lots of little hills. The highest point is Monte Toro, which rises only to 362m (1188ft) and is crowned by a church. Overall, the landscape ranges from rugged and wild to gentle and agricultural. Walking routes tend to be easy in most places.

Occasionally, while walking past lush green pastures grazed by Friesian dairy herds, you may find the countryside surprisingly reminiscent of lowland England!

TREES AND FLOWERS

Menorca's original forests have been harvested and cleared for timber and fuel throughout the ages. The only representatives of naturally regenerating woodland today are found on the steep slopes of the more remote valleys. Some parts of Menorca are densely forested, where tall holm oaks and pines are common. Many areas that were once enclosed and cultivated are reverting to woodland, with wild olive trees and lentisc bushes dominant. Wooded areas may also feature thorny scrub and ivy, broom and tall heather, and where light penetrates the woodland canopy there is an abundance of other plants.

Flowering plants vary enormously, ranging from dense, prickly 'pin-cushion' socarrells, which sprout tiny flowers, to cistus, rock-rose and capers, which produce extensive displays in spring and early summer.

Aromatic rosemary and lavender are common, along with plants having herbal or medicinal uses, such as camomile. On barren rock, plants are often inconspicuous, cowering in cracks to exploit shade and moisture. Amaryllis and asphodels thrive in rocky, barren places.

In wetland areas and meadows plants compete vigorously, while saltmarsh species cope with high salt levels. Some open hillsides, and also sunny spots inside woods and forests, may be covered with tall pampas-like grass, best referred to by its Menorquí name of *càrritx*. Spring is the best time to see flowering plants at their best. In high summer the landscape looks parched, and only in late autumn or winter does it turn green once again, ready for the next display of springtime colours.

The Camí de Son Xoriguer, between Binisafullet and Llucmaçanes (Walk 5)

17

Clockwise from left: Asphodels grow profusely in old abandoned fields all over Menorca; rock-roses often grow among pines; juniper berries are used to flavour Menorcan gin, but not the ones growing on the island.

Walkers passing shallow seas often spot what appear to be grassy meadows underwater. The 'grass' is actually *Posidonia oceanica* – a remarkably important species because it provides food and shelter for a wealth of marine life. However, when rough seas cause masses of posidonia to pile up onto the beaches, it smells awful as it rots. Strange spherical objects that look like coconuts may often be washed ashore, and these are also parts of this plant.

A guide to Mediterranean flowers will help to identify species around Menorca. Well over five per cent of flowering plants are endemic to Menorca, but more than ten per cent of flowering plants have been introduced to the island. The majority of species are Mediterranean stock, common to many other locations.

BIRDS

The premier bird-watching area on Menorca is the Parc Natural de s'Albufera des Grau, on the eastern side of the island. A visitor centre (tel 971-356303), offers plenty of information about species that can be spotted, and there are hides available, overlooking a lagoon surrounded by reeds and bushes. The main species include mallard, coot, moorhen, grebes and pochard.

The cliff coastline is populated by a variety of gulls, as well as cormorants, storm petrels and Mediterranean and Balearic shearwaters. Wooded areas are noted for wood pigeons and turtle doves, while bushy scrub features a variety of finches, warblers and blackbirds. Cattle egrets may be seen among grazing cattle. Birds of prey range from the Egyptian vulture and booted eagle to kestrels, red kites, peregrines and owls. Ospreys are only very rarely seen.

The environmental organisation GOB Menorca can offer plenty of information about the birdlife of Menorca, but their website is in Catalan only: www.gobmenorca. com. They manage the *Centre de la Naturaleza de Menorca*, on Carrer Malloca in Ferreries, which is usually open on Saturdays.

ANIMALS

With the exception of bats, it is likely that nearly all the mammals represented on Menorca were introduced by humans. Most are protected and include small rodents such as dormice and shrews, and larger mammals such as hedgehogs, weasels and pine martens. Rats and rabbits are also present. There are Menorcan varieties of farm animals, including cows, horses, sheep and hens, but the dairy industry is dominated by Friesian herds.

Reptiles include three species of snake, which are rarely encountered. Hermann's tortoises were introduced to the island and can be found almost everywhere, while terrapins occupy certain pools. The Balearic lizard is native, but its strongholds are restricted to small islets dotted around Menorca. Other species of lizards are more widespread, and geckos may be spotted at night. Amphibians include the tree frog and green toad. The most notable insects are butterflies, but cicadas and grasshoppers chirp and whir noisily among the vegetation.

PROTECTED AREAS

The whole island of Menorca was declared a World Biosphere Reserve in 1993. There are over 600 such reserves across the world, including three in England, three in Scotland and one in Wales. They are protected, monitored and managed as demonstration areas for different ecosystems in order to encourage sustainable development.

The 'core area' of the reserve, the Parc Natural de s'Albufera des Grau, was designated in 1995, and this also encompasses the sea off the east coast. The Reserva Marina del Nord de Menorca was established to the north of the island in 1999. Almost half of the island, including most of the coastline, was granted special protection as a 'buffer zone'. Even those parts of the

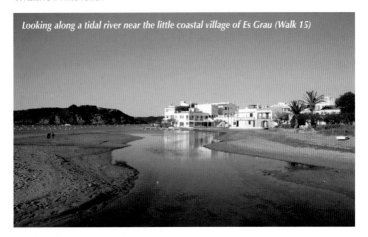

Looking along a tidal river near the little coastal village of Es Grau (Walk 15)

island which aren't specifically protected are still regarded as a 'transition zone' within the Biosphere Reserve.

WHEN TO GO

The best times to walk in Menorca are spring and autumn, but especially spring if you have an interest in wild flowers, or want to see the island at its most colourful. High summer, in July and August, is a very busy time and many walkers would find it too hot to be enjoyable. Winter is generally mild, but it can occasionally be cold, grey and wet. This need not be a problem, but when the ground is wet the clay is often sticky and slippery underfoot. Deep puddles may form on rutted paths and tracks, and some streams may need to be forded. Snow is exceptionally rare and seldom lies for any length of time.

Once on Menorca, the daily weather forecast is easily checked by looking at a copy of the local newspaper, the *Menorca Diario Insular*. The *El Tiempo* page is easily understood as it uses obvious weather symbols.

ACCOMMODATION

Where you choose to base yourself will depend on when you visit Menorca, and how you plan to explore it. If you are planning to use public transport it would be sensible to stay in one of the main centres such as Maó (Mahón) or Ciutadella; however, if you are hiring a car, the island is so small that you will be able to reach your selection of routes from pretty much anywhere, so the seaside resorts will be as practical as the cities.

Menorca has long been sold as a package holiday destination, which means there are plenty of bargains available if you're on a budget, especially in the resorts on the south coast. Outside of the peak summer season and festivals, there is no need to book accommodation in advance. There are enough lodgings available all year round in centres such a Maó, Ciutadella, Fornells on the north coast and Es Mercadal in the middle of the island to suit visiting walkers who want to move from place to place.

Some of the resorts are mostly closed for business outside summer and many of them only have summer bus services. Tourist information offices supply a helpful low-season accommodation list and websites such as www.visitmenorca.com cover all types of accommodation across the island.

Menorca looks wonderful for 'wild camping', but this is illegal, even though it does happen in some popular locations. There are campsites near Biniparratx, Son Bou and Sa Talaia, but these are not located conveniently near the walking routes in this guidebook.

HEALTH AND SAFETY

There are no particular dangers for walkers in Menorca. Naturally, care must be taken near cliffs and beside the sea. Sun protection is advised throughout the year, and sufficient food and drink must be carried when there are no open shops, cafés or bars along the route. Most of the roads followed in this guide are quiet, or have good pavements, but it is always wise to keep an eye on the traffic. Many of the paths used in this guidebook are

Menorca is generally easy to explore on foot, but there are several low hills and rugged paths

also available to mountain bikers and horse riders, and it is wise to step to one side and let them pass.

If you require medication, take adequate supplies with you. Pharmacies can advise in case of minor ailments, while for medical emergencies, phone 061. If a doctor or a trip to a hospital is required, European citizens should present their European Health Insurance Card, which may help to offset the cost of certain treatments.

LANGUAGE

There are two official languages in Menorca: Spanish and Catalan. Catalan is spoken from Andorra to Valencia, as well as on the Balearic Islands. Menorquí is a dialect of Catalan and includes words of French and Arabic origin. No one expects visitors to learn Catalan, let alone Menorquí, and any Spanish you may learn is readily understood on Menorca. Many people in the main resorts and large hotels speak English, German and other languages but this may not be the case in small villages and in the countryside. See Appendix B for basic phrases and useful words in English, Spanish and Catalan and Appendix C for a topographical glossary for use with maps.

MONEY

The Euro is the currency of Menorca. Large denomination Euro notes are difficult to use for small purchases, so avoid the €500 and €200 notes

A solitary white house near Cala de sa Torreta (Walk 15)

The little city of Maó (Mahón) offers the biggest range of services on Menorca

altogether, and avoid the €100 notes if you can. The smaller denominations, €50, €20, €10 and €5, are fine. Coins come in €2 and €1. Small denomination coins come in values of 50c, 20c, 10c, 5c, 2c and 1c. Carry small change for use on the buses. Banks and ATMs are mentioned in route descriptions if further supplies of cash are needed. Many accommodation providers will accept major credit and debit cards, as will large supermarkets; however, small bars, shops and cafés deal only in cash.

COMMUNICATIONS

Menorca has efficient communications systems. The postal system is as good as anywhere else in Europe. There are telephone kiosks dotted around the towns and villages, and mobile phones get a good signal in most urban or elevated locations. However, signals are poor or non-existent in some deep valleys, as well as along some more remote stretches of the northern coastline.

GETTING TO MENORCA

By air

Flights from UK airports to Menorca mainly operate in the summer season, from May to October. Budget operators include Jet2 www.jet2.com, Monarch www.monarch.co.uk and Ryanair www.ryanair.com, and flights are mainly from the London airports, Birmingham and Manchester. There are some flights from a dozen other regional airports. For the rest of the year the choice of airports, airlines and dates on which flights operate is limited. However, this can be overcome by flying via mainland Spain or neighbouring Mallorca, changing onto year-round flights to Menorca operated by Iberia www.iberia.com, Spanair www.spanair.com and Vuelair www.vuelair.com. It is possible to start walking directly from the airport arrivals hall, to see an amazing prehistoric site and then head straight onto quiet country lanes, simply by following Walk 6.

By road or rail

Few travellers consider an overland journey to Menorca, but the Mediterranean ports of Barcelona and Valencia are served by trains and buses. For coach travel check Eurolines, www.eurolines.com, or for trains check www.renfe.es. Driving overland is a very time-consuming approach, but might suit those living in southern Spain.

By sea

There are two main sea approaches to Menorca: the shortest are ferries from Mallorca, and the longest are from mainland Spain. The most regular are from Alcúdia (Mallorca) and Barcelona (Spain) to Ciutadella, operated by Baleària www.balearia.com. The Alcúdia to Ciutadella route is also served by Iscomar www.iscomar.com. Acciona Trasmediterránea serves Maó from Palma (Mallorca), Barcelona and Valencia (Spain).

GETTING AROUND MENORCA

Taking or hiring a car

Taking a car to Menorca may not be a good idea. However, some walkers may wish to use a car in order to have a personalised backup service. If so, choose a good navigator to meet you at intervals along your chosen routes. Some of the one-day walks in this book are linear, rather than circular. The GR223, or Camí de Cavalls, is linear too, and returning to a parked car is inconvenient. Cars can be hired in advance, or on arrival at the airport, or it can be arranged through most hotels.

An impressive network of footpaths and cycleways has been developed around Menorca

Bus services

Menorca has a splendid bus service between 1 May and 31 October, covering the peak summer period, when most settlements and resorts can be reached. During the low season, a reduced bus service operates, but this is perfectly adequate as long as you study the timetables carefully.

Winter buses run regularly between Maó, Alaior, Es Mercadal, Ferreries and Ciutadella. The airport, Es Castell, Sant Lluís, Sant Climent, Cala en Porter, Es Migjorn Gran and Fornells can all be reached from Maó. Cala en Bosc, Cala Blanca, sa Caleta, Cala en Forcat and Es Migjorn Gran can all be reached from Ciutadella. There are also buses running between Es Mercadel and Fornells, and between Fornells and Arenal d'en Castell.

Different bus companies operate along different routes, and most timetables can be checked at the bus station in Maó. Transportes Menorca (TMSA) www.tmsa.es, Torres www.e-torres.es and Autos Fornells www.autosfornells. com all post timetables online, and up-to-date bus timetables for the whole island are also printed in the local newspaper, *Menorca Diario Insular*, on the *Transportes Autobuses* page.

The only real bus station on Menorca is in Maó. When leaving it to access walking routes in the city, simply follow pedestrian signposts from the Plaça de S'Esplanada to the 'Port' or 'Centre Històric'. To return to the bus station from the city centre, follow signposts for 'Estació d'autobusos'.

Buses from Ciutadella operate from two different locations so, if changing there, be sure to ask the driver from where the next bus departs. In other towns and villages, if the bus stop isn't evident, ask someone for directions to the *parada* (bus stop).

Taxis

Taxis are available in all towns and most villages throughout Menorca, usually close to the main squares. Cars operate under the aegis of the Asociacion Menorquina De Radio Taxis (tel 971-367111). The telephone number covers the whole island, and all you need to do is to state where you are and where you want to go, and leave it to the operator to locate an available car. The green sign *Lliure/ Libre* means 'free' and any taxi displaying this can be flagged down. In case of difficulty ask your hotel, or a roadside bar, to call one for you. Offer a couple of Euros if they demur. A general rule of thumb is that a long taxi journey will cost five times more than the bus fare. If three or four walkers share a taxi, the individual cost is close to the bus fare for the same journey. Tips of ten per cent are customary.

WHAT TO TAKE

Even in winter on Menorca, walkers need take no more than they would take for a summer trip in Britain. The weather will probably be warm, and might be very hot and sunny, so take clothing that will protect against sunburn, as well as sunscreen and a hat. On the other hand, if it rains, be prepared with lightweight waterproofs. Footwear is a personal choice, and walkers wear everything from heavy boots to lightweight sandals. However, bear in mind that the ground can sometimes be rocky or stony underfoot and occasionally steep, and after a spell of rain some parts can get quite wet and muddy.

WAYMARKING AND ACCESS

Most routes available for public use around Menorca are exceptionally well waymarked and signposted. The long-distance GR223, or Camí de Cavalls, is particularly well-marked. GR stands for *gran recorrido*, and the route is flashed red/white in the usual European fashion. The waymarking is particularly helpful where the route passes through woods or scrub, where it is not possible to see far ahead; however, it is easier to lose the route in towns and villages where

there are lots of distractions. There are also two waymarked PR (*pequeño recorrido*) routes, PR-IB-Me 1 and PR-IB-Me 2, which are flashed yellow/white, with a particular emphasis on archaeology.

Many walking routes are also marked as cycleways, so keep your eyes and ears open, and hope that any mountain bikers on the trails also have your well-being in mind! Only a couple of routes cross private property, where walkers have been tolerated for many years, but bear in mind that the landowners could withdraw access at any time. Walk 10, through the Barranc de sa Cova, and Walk 15, around Sa Torreta, are examples.

MAPS

The best map for exploring Menorca on foot is the Editorial Alpina Menorca *(Left to right): signs on the PR-IB-Me 2 trail (Walk 7); marker post on the Camí de Cavalls; signs at a junction of the Camí de Cavalls*

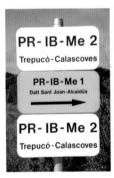  

sheet, at a scale of 1:50,000 (www.
editorialalpina.com). This highlights
the long-distance Camí de Cavalls (in
green) and many other walking routes,
as well as showing the intricate network
of roads and farm tracks around the
island. Its detail is equal to what walkers
would expect of the Ordnance Survey
Landranger series of maps in Britain.

Extracts from the Editorial Alpina
map have been reproduced in this
guidebook by kind permission of the
publishers. These are fine for each of
the walking routes, but if you want to
see how all the routes relate to each
other, then either obtain the complete
map in advance of a visit, or look out
for it on Menorca, where it is widely
available and widely used by walkers.
UK stockists include Stanfords (12-14
Long Acre, London, WC2E 9BR, tel 020
7836 1321, www.stanfords.co.uk) and
The Map Shop (15 High Street, Upton-
upon-Severn, WR8 0HJ, tel 01684
593146, www.themapshop.co.uk).

FOOD AND DRINK

There are plenty of restaurants, cafés,
bars and shops in the towns and villages around Menorca, so it is usually easy to obtain food and drink.
Even some remote beaches have a
small café/bar or restaurant. However,
there are some walks that have little
or nothing, so it is always a good idea
to carry enough food and drink for
the day. See Appendix B for food and
drink items.

TOURIST INFORMATION OFFICES

There are five tourist information
offices around Menorca. They offer
plenty of local information and might
help with accommodation searches,
attractions, opening times, bus timetables and so on. They should have
information about the long-distance
Camí de Cavalls, as well as knowledge of nearby walking and cycling
opportunities.
- Airport Arrivals Hall,
  tel 971-157115
- Plaça de S'Esplanada, Maó,
  tel 971-367415
- Moll de Levant, Port de Maó,
  tel 971-355952
- Plaça de la Catedral, Ciutadella,
  tel 971-382693
- Casa del Contramaestre, Fornells,
  tel 971-158430

EMERGENCIES

If emergency assistance is required
on land, phone 112 and explain
the nature of the incident to an
English-speaking operator. If a rescue is required, a response might be
mounted by the fire service (bombers) or the police. The police can
be contacted directly, either phoning 092 for the Policía Municipal,
091 for the Policía Nacional, or 062
for the Guardia Civil. Alternatively,
for a medical emergency, phone
061. For sea rescues, phone 112 or
900-202202.

These walkers are evidently backpacking, but where do they intend to camp, since it is illegal to camp wild?

USING THIS GUIDE

There are 20 one-day walks in this guidebook; 16 of these are spread around most parts of Menorca, but are particularly concentrated within easy reach of Maó. The Coast to Coast route across the island from Maó to Ciutadella, a total of 71km (44½ miles), is divided into four one-day stages. Most walks are easy, but sometimes there are short, steep, rocky or stony slopes, and some areas are densely vegetated, where it is possible to become disorientated. Many of the walks, not just the Coast to Coast ones, link with adjacent walks, so that it is possible to extend the distance.

The only thing that really makes a walk difficult on Menorca is distance, particularly in the peak summer period when it is very hot. There is enough information in the introduction to each day's walk for readers to choose walks that are appropriate to their abilities.

The long-distance GR223, or Camí de Cavalls, completely encircles Menorca, and while many stretches can be completed as simple day-walks, walking the full circuit day after day requires a lot of planning. See the separate introduction to this long-distance walk later in the guidebook.

Note that the **spellings** of place names used in the route descriptions match the spellings that readers will encounter while in Menorca, on street signs and the like. In some places these do not correspond exactly with those that appear on the official map, and therefore on the route maps. However, the differences are small and places easy to identify.

DAY WALKS

The rugged cliff coast path runs past Cala Fustam and Cala Escorxada (Walk 9)

29

WALK 1

Maó and Es Castell

Start	Plaça d'Espanya, Maó
Finish	Plaça de S'Arraval Vella, Es Castell
Distance	8km (5 miles)
Total Ascent/Descent	100m (330ft)
Time	2hrs 30min
Terrain	Easy walking along coastal roads, promenades and narrow cliff paths.
Refreshment	Plenty of choice in Maó, Es Castell and Cales Fonts.
Public transport	Regular daily buses link Maó and Es Castell, extending to Sol de l'Est in summer.

The built-up southern shore of Port de Maó, between the city of Maó and neighbouring Es Castell, is more interesting than maps might suggest. There are fine, short cliff-top paths, lovely little coves and views of Fortalesa de la Mola, the fortified headland guarding the harbour. This coastal walk can be followed instead of the first part of the long-distance GR223, or Camí de Cavalls, which simply follows a main road directly from Maó to Es Castell.

There are many ways to leave the Plaça d'Espanya in the centre of **Maó**, and a street map (such as the one at the front of this guide) will be useful. Walk down the bendy road, Costa de ses Voltes, or take a short-cut down broad flights of stone steps. Reach the shore of

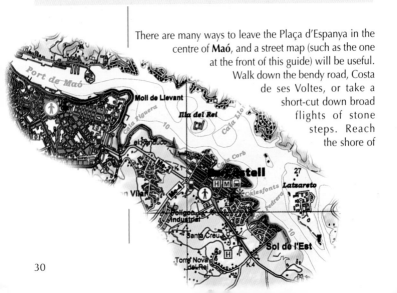

Maó's waterfront reflected in the waters of Cala Figuera

Port de Maó beside ticket booths for a variety of short cruises. ▶

Turn right and follow a generous path between the sea and the coastal road. A multitude of boats are moored alongside, while across the road are plenty of bars and restaurants. Swing right round the Moll de Llevant, pass the Casino Marítim and follow the road round the small inlet of **Cala Figuera**. The buildings are rather shabby here, and the road ends suddenly at a slipway.

Just before the slipway, climb steps beside an electricity transformer tower. Turn left and climb more steps past houses. A narrow, well-trodden cliff-top path squeezes between bushes of *càrritx* and euphorbia, and the surface is often worn to bare limestone. ▶ Houses lie ahead, so join a track to approach them, then continue straight along Carrer Gran into **Es Castell**.

Turn left down Carrer Cala Corb to reach the cliff-bound harbour of **Cala Corb**. Climb steps on the right to reach the cliff-top and continue along a broad, brick-paved path called Miranda de Cala Corb. Turn right along Carrer de Bellavista, losing views of the sea, then turn left down Carrer Sant Ignasi, passing below the Hotel

Cruises include the 'Glass Bottom Boats', circuits of the harbour and the Fortalesa de la Mola.

Note the island of Illa del Rei, where the British built a substantial hospital.

Barrack-style buildings above Cala Corb in the village of Es Castell.

Hamilton. Follow a fine   brick-paved promenade, later turning right to reach the inlet of **Cales Fonts** (bars, restaurants, boats offering harbour tours).

At the head of the inlet, either follow a wooden walkway below a cliff, and later climb steps up the cliff, or head inland, turn sharp left and pick up a cliff-top path that enjoys fine views of the harbour. Either way, continue along the cliff-top path, which is narrow and unfenced. Steps later drop to a rocky shore popular with fishermen, then climb back to the cliff-top. Pass wooden decking and climb a few more steps, following the cliff path to the head of another inlet at **Cala Pedrera**.

Climb concrete steps beside the Bar Restaurante Sol Naciente and turn left along a road. Watch for a narrow path on the left, squeezing past broom bushes to continue along the low cliffs at **Sol de l'Est**. The path passes a housing development and crosses a bouldery wall into fields, but cannot be followed much further. Enjoy the views across to the Fortalesa de la Mola, then retrace your steps until a short concrete track can be followed inland.

Turn left along a road, the Passeig Marítim, which bends right and climbs, becoming the Avinguda del Port. Reach a crossroads where the long distance Camí de Cavalls passes (see GR223 – Stage 1). Turn right to follow a broad pavement beside the road, straight back to **Es Castell**. Finish at the bus stop on Plaça de S'Arraval Vella. ▶

A narrow cliff-top path can be followed away from Cales Fonts

A bus can be caught here back to Maó.

WALK 2
Cala de Sant Esteve and s'Algar

Start	Plaça de S'Arraval Vella, Es Castell
Finish	Bar Via Maris, Alcalfar
Distance	8km (5 miles)
Total Ascent/Descent	110m (360ft)
Time	4hrs
Terrain	Easy at first, mostly along roads, then difficult, rough and rocky afterwards, with a few short, steep and rocky ascents and descents.
Refreshment	Bars and restaurants available in Es Castell, s'Algar and Alcalfar.
Public transport	Regular daily buses link Maó with Es Castell. Summer buses serve Sol de l'Est, s'Algar and Alcalfar.

This walk follows roads from Es Castell to Cala de Sant Esteve, in common with the GR223, or Camí de Cavalls. However, when the GR223 moves inland, this walk follows the rugged cliffs onwards as closely as possible. Paths can be vague in places and the ground is often rough and rocky. The rewards for the effort are views of fine cliffs and access to a splendid rocky inlet at Caló de Rafalet. A short walk at the end links s'Algar and Alcalfar.

This walk starts at **Es Castell** (hotels, shops, bar restaurants) or if summer buses are in operation, it is possible to start at nearby Sol de l'Est, but this saves less than 1km (½ mile) of road-walking, so it is neither here nor there. Leave the bus stop at Plaça de S'Arraval Vella and continue along the main road from a roundabout. ◀

Although there is a GR223 signpost across the roundabout, there is no pavement on that side.

The road has a broad pavement alongside and eventually reaches a crossroads. **Sol de l'Est** lies to the left, but walk straight ahead as signposted for Fort de Marlborough, passing a cemetery. Reach a signposted junction and note Castillo de San Felipe ahead, an occupied 18th-century fort, but turn right instead. Walk along and down the road, passing fields, then fork right down a broad path flanked by bushes. This is bendy and cobbled

The attractive bendy and cobbled path down to Cala de Sant Esteve

and avoids using the road to reach the narrow inlet of **Cala de Sant Esteve**.

Turn right to follow the road round the head of the inlet, passing cave houses and the cave-like entrance to Fort de Marlborough – an early 18th century British redoubt. ▶ Continue along the road to the mouth of the inlet, stepping down onto a rocky platform. See where blocks of stone were quarried and cut, leaving level areas and stepped profiles. Pick a way round the cliffs, and climb up rock steps to continue along a trodden path. Later, parts of the cliff are breaking off, so **keep clear of the edge**.

The GR223, Stage 1, leaves Cala de Sant Esteve by a different route.

Head for a prominent stone tower which can be entered by climbing a set of bent metal steps.

The view from the **Torre d'en Penjat** stretches from the mouth of Port de Maó and its many fortifications, inland to Monte Toro, the highest point on Menorca.

Thick walls flank the tower, so follow one of these directly down towards the sea. Turn right through a gap with steps to continue. There are two sizeable houses above the rocky shore, surrounded by walled fields. A trodden path keeps seaward of these walls, although it isn't particularly clear where it crosses bare limestone. First, squeeze between a wall and tamarisk bushes, then follow a trodden path, passing a livestock shelter and a ruin.

Follow the path until a small rocky inlet is reached at **Caló des Vi Blanc**, where the wall turns a corner. There is a stone step-stile in the corner, offering a way over the wall, if squeezing past the wall above the inlet doesn't appeal. Either way, the path onwards is vague, rising rockily and stonily, passing through a gap in a wall. Use the wall as a guide ahead, but feel free to search for the least rugged ground

Massive boulders litter the shore near the point of sa Cigonya

underfoot. Turn round a point at **sa Cigonya** to reach a curious small stone building. ▸

Follow the wall onwards to a little inlet, and look carefully to spot a rocky path climbing to the top of the cliffs. There is a lot of rock and scrub around, so find and follow a vaguely trodden path. If in doubt, then keep the cliff edge in view, but don't get too close to it, and continue carefully across bare and broken rock. A wall reaches the cliff edge, and a stone step-stile crosses it. Follow the path downhill, passing carefully around an inlet where the cliffs overhang. ▸

Pass between the end of a wall and a cliff edge, where the path squeezes between bushes, and walk uphill to go through a gateway gap in a wall. There is a slight dip along the cliff edge at **Penyal Alt des Sòtil**, with lots of euphorbia bushes dotted around. Limestone pavement reaches the cliff edge; then there is a stone stile over a wall. Pass through a cleared, grassy, stony space surrounded by bushy scrub. A trodden path squeezes into the bushes and runs downhill, rocky underfoot. Do not go down the cliffs using a trodden path, but head inland a bit to pick up a wide, trodden earth path instead. Follow

The coast features masses of rocky slabs that have been flipped over by mighty storms.

Marvel at the house-sized boulders in the sea.

The narrow, rocky inlet of Caló de Rafalet is reached before s'Algar.

The GR223, Stage 1, can be followed onwards.

this carefully downhill, crossing steep rock, continuing down to a tiny sandy beach hemmed in by wonderfully attractive cliffs at **Caló de Rafalet**.

There are two ways to leave this inlet. One is to walk directly inland, up a well-wooded valley, linking with the GR223, then turn left for Alcalfar, or right to return to Cala de Sant Esteve. The other way is to climb back from the sand, over rocks, and as soon as the path levels out, turn left and climb up the steep, rocky wooded slope. A winding path leaves the woods and rises on a more open slope of scrub and bushes. A stone step-stile crosses a wall close to some houses.

Walk down a road running parallel to the cliffs. The rock alongside is savagely eroded and generally too difficult to walk across. When the road later turns right inland through the resort of **s'Algar** (hotels, shops, bars, restaurants, summer buses, taxis), go down Carrer d'es Sol and turn right to pick up another coastal road with a promenade path and palm trees alongside. Stay on the promenade and pass seawards of s'Algar Diving, passing a curious blend of mock-paved concrete and low rocks.

A notice reads 'Playa Beach Strand Alcaufar' and a path follows a wall past rampant mixed bushy scrub. Squeeze between a couple of houses and turn right up a road, Carrer de Xaloc, into the village of **Alcalfar**. Turn left to reach a junction, then turn right to reach a bus stop opposite the Bar Via Maris. ◄

WALK 3
Maó and Trebalúger

Start/Finish	Plaça d'Espanya, Maó
Distance	15km (9½ miles)
Total Ascent/Descent	100m (330ft)
Time	5hrs
Terrain	Mostly gentle roads, tracks and paths, with one short stony stretch.
Refreshment	Plenty of choice in Maó.
Public transport	Plenty of bus services to and from Maó.

The city of Maó quickly gives way to gentle countryside, where drystone-walled roads and tracks runs through fields and link quiet little villages. This route visits interesting talaiots at Trebalúger and Trepucó in a circuit from the centre of Maó. By studying maps, quiet lanes can be identified to link this walk with Walks 4 and 5. This allows longer walks to be created, taking in more villages and ancient sites, with no need to return to Maó.

There are many ways to leave the Plaça d'Espanya in **Maó**, and a street map (such as the one at the front of this guide) will prove useful. Walk into the adjoining Plaça del Carme and keep right of the large building, Claustre del Carme. Turn left at the Plaça del Princep to walk through Plaça de la Miranda. ▶

A fine viewpoint overlooks the inlet of Port de Maó.

Turn right to follow a road along the top of a cliff and/or wall. This is the Costa de la Miranda, becoming the Passeig Marítim. At times there is a path running parallel that can be used. The road turns right and passes the Casino Marítim, overlooking the small inlet of **Cala Figuera**. Turn left along a road to reach a roundabout. Turn left again, not down the road called Costa de Corea, but along a paved path that continues above the inlet. This leads to the busy **Me-2 road**. Turn left along it, then quickly right along the Camí Verd.

Watch for a narrow path on the left, which leads to steps climbing quickly to another road, the Camí de

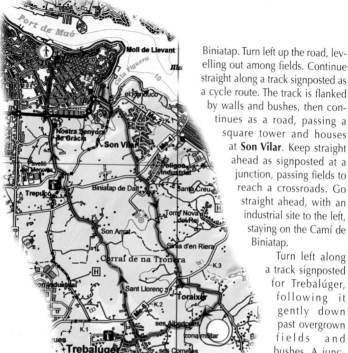

Biniatap. Turn left up the road, levelling out among fields. Continue straight along a track signposted as a cycle route. The track is flanked by walls and bushes, then continues as a road, passing a square tower and houses at **Son Vilar**. Keep straight ahead as signposted at a junction, passing fields to reach a crossroads. Go straight ahead, with an industrial site to the left, staying on the Camí de Biniatap.

Turn left along a track signposted for Trebalúger, following it gently down past overgrown fields and bushes. A junction is reached where our route, the Camí de Biniatap, heads right. ◄ When a road is reached at **Toraixer**, cross over and follow a track past houses, keeping left and quickly joining another road. Turn right along this bendy road, which later makes a pronounced bend to the right. Turn right along a track called the Camí Fosc.

The Camí de Rafal heads left.

The track rises and falls, worn to lumpy bedrock, and then it narrows. Later it broadens to become a gentle track again; follow it straight ahead, ignoring other tracks to right and left. Keep straight ahead as signposted along a tarmac road, reaching a junction with the Camí de Rafalet in the village of **Trebalúger**.

Turn right to reach another junction, then turn left along Carrer de sa Torre. Pass the torre, which is a square

white building. Keep straight ahead at junctions until Sant Lluís is signposted to the left. However, don't turn left, but turn right instead, then turn left up the Camí d'es Talaiot. A gate on the left leads to the **Talaiot de Trebalúger**.

The Talaiot de Trebalúger is one of the oldest talaiots on Menorca

> The bouldery structure sitting on a rocky outcrop is **Talaiot de Trebalúger**, one of the oldest *talaiots* on Menorca, dating from around 1500–100BC. It occupies the site of an earlier structure. The view from the top, barely rising above 50m (165ft), takes in much of south-east Menorca, including parts of Maó, the headland of La Mola, the villages of Trebalúger and Sant Lluís and the airport.

Retrace your steps back into Trebalúger via Carrer de sa Torre and turn left along the Camí de Rafalet, passing a supermarket. Cross the busy **Me-6 road** to continue along a track, the Camí de Trepucó a Trebalúger. This passes the 'Menorca Clearance Centre' and later narrows dramatically. Now little more than a path, the surface is covered with loose lumps of rock for a while. A firmer

The Poblat de Trepucó is one of the largest talaiotic settlements in Menorca

stretch meanders through fields, eventually reaching a junction with another track. Keep left and join a road on a corner.

Turn right as signposted for Maó and follow the road straight ahead past other roads and tracks around **Son Amar**. A series of roads is signposted for 'Poblat de Trepucó', so follow these one after another, always turning left. However, after passing a ceramics studio, it is also possible to take a short cut up a path on the left, called Camí des Moro, then turn right along a road to reach **Trepucó**.

A massive, boulder-walled talaiot, **Poblat de Trepucó**, dominates Trepucó; at least four of these structures were built on this site, which is one of the largest settlements of its type on Menorca. Alongside is a tall T-shaped *taula*, standing in an enclosure flanked by stone pillars. Also visible are house foundations, and there are other foundations in nearby fields. The whole site was excavated in the 1930s by British archaeologist Margaret Murray.

Walk down the road, the Camí de Trepucó, then decide whether to turn right or left. By turning right along the Camí Verd, the Me-2 road can be reached at the head of Cala Figuera. From there, the earlier steps of the day can be retraced back into the city. Turning left, however, leads down to another junction, where a right turn leads down to a large cemetery at **Nostra Senyora de Gràcia**. Cross the Me-2 at a roundabout and follow the Carrer de Gràcia straight into Maó. Turning left at the end of this road leads to Plaça Reial, where a right turn leads to Plaça del Carme and Plaça d'Espanya in **Maó**.

WALK 4
Sant Lluís and Biniancolla

Start/Finish	Sant Lluís
Distance	12km (7½ miles)
Total Ascent/Descent	75m (245ft)
Time	3hrs 30min
Terrain	Easy walking along roads and tracks, mostly at gentle gradients past fields, coast and scrub-covered areas.
Refreshment	Plenty of choice in Sant Lluís. Bar/restaurants in Biniancolla and Torret.
Public transport	Regular daily buses serve Sant Lluís from Maó. Summer buses serve Cala Biniancolla.

Sant Lluís is an interesting large village, well worth exploring; its streets are laid out grid-fashion, reminding visitors that it was once a garrison town. Roads and tracks can be followed southwards to the coastal resort of Biniancolla, then northwards to return to Sant Lluís. Two old towers can be seen on the return journey: Torre de sa Vigia and a tower that gives its name to the little village of Torret.

Leave **Sant Lluís** by following the main road as if heading for the south coast. There are two ways to continue, which join up before long. Either walk to a roundabout and take the road left, signposted for Biniancolla, using the red cycleway and walkway alongside, or turn left before the roundabout and walk down the Camí de Consell; head gently uphill and turn left at **es Consell**. Continue gently downhill and turn right. The road is still named as the Camí des Consell; walk down it, then up to the main road at a crossroads. Cross over the main road, then turn left along the red cycleway and walkway, followed in the alternative route, near **Torret**.

Follow the main road gently uphill and round a bend, reaching another crossroads and a cycleway mapboard. Turn right and follow the **Camí Vell de Biniancolla**, which runs gently downhill as a tarmac road flanked by

Views stretch from the headland of La Mola to the village of Torret and the highest point on Menorca, Monte Toro.

The view is of a lighthouse on the island of Illa de l'Aire.

The Bar Restaurante La Baia lies across the road, beside the inlet of Cala Biniancolla.

walls, fields and a couple of farms. After passing a gate, it continues as a broad track flanked by walls and fields, heading gently downhill and uphill, now with wild olives alongside. There is a sewage works to the left, and on the crest of the track at **sa Serreta**, a concrete picnic table and benches are available. ◄

The track runs gently down past bushy scrub and rocky ground, passing a picnic site and a 'vista panoràmica' sign. ◄ The track becomes metalled again, dropping more steeply, with views of houses along the coast, both left and right. Pass another picnic table and continue down to a gateway and road junction, where there are signposts and a cycleway mapboard. Walk straight down the road, Carrer de sa Devallada, reaching another road junction and bus stops near **Son Ganxo**. ◄

Turn right to follow the coastal road called the Passeig Marítim. One stretch of it is free of development, becoming Carrer de S'Oronella, passing the Restaurante en Caragol on the way to **Biniancolla**. Walk along a broad pavement, passing a little rocky inlet

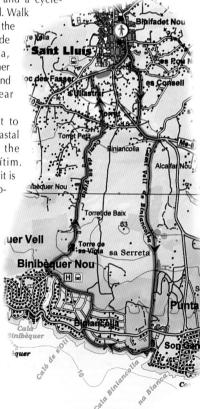

Drystone walls enclose small fields all around the village of Sant Lluís

The Camí de sa Vigia runs inland to the little village of Torret

and a small white hut or house. When a road junction is reached, turn right, uphill and inland, as signposted for 'Torret de Baix'. Walk through a roundabout to follow Carrer de sa Cadernera uphill. There aren't many houses, just masses of wild olives and lentisc awaiting future construction projects.

The road bends left at the top, and by walking straight ahead, it descends and curves round a wooded slope. Reach a few houses and a signpost at a junction on the outskirts of **Binibèquer Nou**. Turn right up the Camí de sa Morena Perillosa, making a short, steep climb, then turn right as signposted up a track called the **Camí de sa Vigia**. Pass dense wild olives and lentisc and broom scrub. Follow the winding track and keep left of three features: a waterworks, the **Torre de sa Vigia**, and the red house of Sa Vigia.

Go through a gateway and head downhill, with bare limestone poking through the track surface. Turn left at a junction and follow a tarmac road full of pot-holes and strewn with gravel. Pass fields and houses around **Torret de Baix**, as well as wooded and scrubby areas, and ascend gently. There is a view of a tower, or *torre*, before reaching a road junction in the little village of **Torret**.

Turn left up the Camí de Torret, then turn right down the narrow Camí de la Coixa, past the Restaurante Pan y Vino. Walk down the grassy, walled track that winds and serves a number of properties, becoming stony and gritty as it continues down to a main road near **s'Ullastrar**. Turn right, and as soon as an opportunity presents itself, step down to the right into a little pine forest where there is a fitness trail. Go through a subway beneath the main road and walk up to a roundabout, then follow the main road straight into **Sant Lluís**.

WALK 5
Llucmaçanes and Binissafúllet

Start/Finish	Església de Sant Gaietà, Llucmaçanes
Distance	12km (7½ miles)
Total Ascent/Descent	50m (165ft)
Time	3hrs 30min
Terrain	Easy walking, mostly along roads and tracks, with a couple of narrow paths. Mostly gentle farmland with fields and some areas of scrub.
Refreshment	Bar restaurant in Llucmaçanes. Bar at Binissafúllet.
Public transport	None, but buses serve the nearby airport and Sant Lluís, which can both be reached by linking with Walk 6.

Llucmaçanes is a quiet and attractive little village near Maó. A figure-of-eight walk can be made from the village, comprising long and short circular walks. The longer circuit takes in the Menorca Cricket Club and a splendid talaiotic settlement at Poblat de Binissafúllet. The shorter circuit links with the waymarked PR-IB-Me 2, followed in Walk 7. Although there are no buses serving Llucmaçanes, Walk 6 also passes through the village, linking the airport and the village of Sant Lluís, which both have regular daily bus services.

Start from the stone church, Església de Sant Gaietà, in **Llucmaçanes** and follow a road, turning left past Llucmaçanes Gran Agroturismo to reach a crossroads. Turn right as signposted for Sant Lluís, following Carrer de sa Font. At the next junction turn right along the Camí de Biniparrell, also signposted for Sant Lluís. Walk gently up the road, passing houses, fields and the 'Terme Municipal de Sant Lluís'. Keep walking straight ahead (Walk 6 turns left for Sant Lluís) up the road which broadens at a junction and mapboard. If required, the Camí de Biniati to the right offers a short cut. Otherwise, keep walking ahead, gently down the road. ▶ Later, the Menorca Cricket Club is reached on the right.

Note the rampant scrub to the left that is a wildlife refuge.

The **Menorca Cricket Club** was founded by British ex-patriots in 1985, and this cricket ground, which claims to be the most beautiful in the Mediterranean, was opened in 1992. The club enjoys what it calls 'competitive village cricket' and has hosted visiting teams from around the world. They also play teams from Mallorca and Ibiza for the Balearic Cup (see **www. menorcacricketclub.com**).

The road rises to a junction with a busy road. Turn right as signposted for **Binissafúllet** and take care as there is no pavement beside the road. A bar is reached at Binissafúllet Vell and opposite is direct access to Poblat de Binissafúllet.

Poblat de Binissafúllet, a talaiotic settlement dating from 1300BC, was partly destroyed during construction of the road. However, much remains to be seen, including its central *talaiot*, and its T-shaped *taula*, which was restored in 1992. The foundations of houses and other structures can be seen around the site.

Either turn right at the adjacent road junction, to follow the Camí de Binissafúllet, or leave the site by an exit directly onto that road, then turn right. Follow the road past houses such as Binisafuet Nou and San Martín. Turn right down a broad walled track called the Camí des Marrocs. The track begins to rise from a 'Finca Privada' notice, so keep right and follow a narrow vegetated walled path that winds between scrub-covered fields. Reach a road bend at the access to Son Marroxet, where

the short-cut comes in from the right, and go straight ahead along the road called **Camí de Biniati**.

When the road turns left, keep straight ahead, gently down a walled path called the Camí de Son Xoriguer. This winds past fields and narrows as it passes a sign for the Camí de Biniati. The path rises gently and very suddenly reaches buildings at **Llucmaçanes**, where a broad, walled track leads to the stone church of Església de Sant Gaietà. ▶

To continue directly onto the shorter circular walk, turn left in the village and quickly reach a road junction, mapboard and cycling signposts. Keep left, in effect straight ahead, along the Camí de Na Ferranda, signposted for Maó. ▶ Pass Cas Vinater, which sells wine, and keep walking until a crossroads is reached. Turn right along the track called **Camí d'en Claudis**, which is part of the waymarked PR-IB-Me 2, followed in Walk 7.

Follow the track past fields, running close to a house, where it becomes grassy and narrower. The track winds gently downhill past more fields, and the narrowest part comes just before it joins a road called the Camí de Baix. Turn right to follow this back to **Llucmaçanes**, and if returning to the church, turn right along Carrer Nou, then left to finish.

The Poblat de Binisafúllet was partly destroyed, but its fine taula remains standing

Walk 6 also follows this track; the airport and regular bus services are nearby.

Hallissy's Bar Restaurante, with tall pines alongside, is open at weekends.

WALK 6
Airport to Sant Lluís

Start	Airport
Finish	Sant Lluís
Distance	6km (3¾ miles)
Total Ascent/Descent	25m (80ft)
Time	2hrs
Terrain	Easy and almost level, following roads, tracks and linking paths past farmland and woodland.
Refreshment	Bar restaurant at the airport. Bar restaurant at Llucmaçanes. Several bars and restaurants at Sant Lluís.
Public transport	Regular daily buses serve both the airport and Sant Lluís from Maó.

There aren't many places where you can walk out of an airport, pass an interesting archaeological site and quickly find yourself following country lanes and paths from village to village. Menorca's airport has a regular bus service, and this walk cuts across country, through the village of Llucmaçanes, to reach the village of Sant Lluís, where there are also regular bus services.

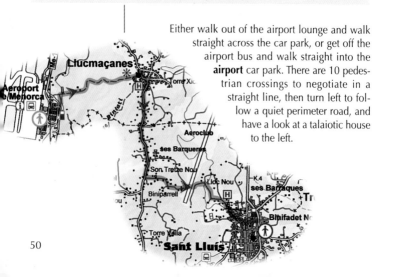

Either walk out of the airport lounge and walk straight across the car park, or get off the airport bus and walk straight into the **airport** car park. There are 10 pedestrian crossings to negotiate in a straight line, then turn left to follow a quiet perimeter road, and have a look at a talaiotic house to the left.

Casa Talaiòtica de Biniparratxet Petit was originally located at the southern end of the airport runway. It was dismantled and rebuilt here in 1995 to allow the airport to develop. The site features a dwelling house with separate rooms. There is a hypostyle room for storage, which was later divided, as well as an open central courtyard, a hearth and a cistern. The house was abandoned after the Roman conquest of Menorca in 123BC.

Doorway into the rebuilt talaiotic house beside the busy airport

Continue along the road and turn right, walking gently down a road flanked by bushes, ending at the Avis rental car pound. The Camí de Tornaltí is marked by a sign, so turn left and it is revealed as a walled path, winding past fields. It leads to a broad track, where a left turn leads quickly to a stone church, Església de Sant Gaietà, and a road in the village of **Llucmaçanes**. ►

Turn right and follow a road, turning left past Llucmaçanes Gran Agroturismo to reach a crossroads. Turn right as signposted for Sant Lluís, following Carrer de sa Font. At the next junction, turn right along the Camí

This church is the start and finish points of Walk 5.

Es Molí de Dalt is a windmill on top of a museum at Sant Lluís

de Biniparrell, also signposted for Sant Lluís. Walk gently up the road, passing houses, fields and a sign for the 'Terme Municipal de Sant Lluís'. Keep walking straight ahead up the road, and take note of two roads on the left. First is Camí des Vidals, and second is Camí de ses Barqueres, where a left turn is made. ▸

Walk 5 continues straight up the road.

At the end of the winding road, continue along a path which soon reaches an old airstrip now used by an Aeroclub. Head slightly left to cross it and be sure to pick up a path on the other side. This is narrow, winding, and well-trodden as it passes bushes, reaching a locked gate and a road. Follow the road ahead and turn right at a junction, where the tarmac broadens considerably at **Lloc Nou**.

The Camí des Lloc Nou leads to the outskirts of the village of **Sant Lluís**; (some accommodation, shops, bars, restaurants, post office, banks with ATMs, buses, taxis) continue straight ahead along the Camí de Binifadet. The road winds past houses, reaching a small car park. Turn left along the Carrer del Duc de Crillon, which leads to a crossroads beside a museum and windmill at Es Molí de Dalt. Walk straight ahead to reach the main road, Avinguda de sa Pau.

Sant Lluís was named in 1761 after King Louis IX of France (Saint Louis, 1214–1270) during the brief French occupation of Menorca. The settlement was developed as a garrison, with its streets laid out in a grid. Although the church, signposted as 'Església', is large, the streets around it are narrow and it is difficult to get a decent view of the structure. The windmill of Es Molí de Dalt is a striking feature, sitting on top of the Museu Etnològic de Sant Lluís.

WALK 7
Maó to Cala en Porter

Start	Plaça d'Espanya, Maó
Finish	Plaça d'en Mevis, Cala en Porter
Distance	23km (14¼ miles)
Total Ascent/Descent	200m (655ft)
Time	7hrs
Terrain	Mostly gentle roads, tracks and paths, through wooded countryside and villages, becoming more rugged towards the end.
Refreshment	Plenty of choice in Maó. Bars and restaurants at El Picadero, Sant Climent, off-route at Son Vitamina, and at Cala en Porter.
Public transport	Regular daily buses serve Maó, Sant Climent, Urbanització Calascoves and Cala en Porter.

The waymarked PR-IB-Me 2 trail runs from Trepucó, on the outskirts of Maó, to Calascoves, close to Cala en Porter. The route passes, or runs close to, a series of interesting archaeological sites, so allow plenty of time to explore them. They include the Poblat de Trepucó, Talaiot de Curnia Vell, Talaiot de Torellonet Vell, Basílica des Fornàs de Torelló, Talaiot de Binicalaf and the Necropolis de Calascoves. If the trail is extended at either end, so that it runs from Maó to Cala en Porter, then both ends link with bus services.

There are many ways to leave the Plaça d'Espanya in **Maó**, and a street map (such as the one at the front of this guide) will prove useful. Walk up through the adjoining Plaça del Carme into Plaça Princep. Follow Carrer del Carme and turn right along the narrow Carrer de Santa Eulàlia. This broadens where there is an old house and a few fields. Turn right and left to follow the Camí des Castell, which leads straight to the edge of the city, to a roundabout on the Me-2 road. Go straight down the main road towards the head of an inlet, **Cala Figuera**.

Turn right to follow another road, Camí Verd, into a valley flanked by quarried cliffs with caves cut into them.

The valley bottom is now agricultural, with walls and terraces made of square-cut blocks of stone. Follow the road up a well-wooded slope. ▶ When a complex road junction is reached, simply turn left up the Camí de Trepucó, also marked as the PR-IB-Me 2 trail and signposted for Poblat de Trepucó.

There are occasional fields tucked away, and the 'Equimar' horse-riding centre to the left.

> A massive, boulder-walled *talaiot*, the **Poblat de Trepucó**, dominates Trepucó; at least four of these structures were built on this site, which is one of the largest settlements of its type on Menorca. Alongside is a tall T-shaped *taula*, standing in an enclosure flanked by stone pillars. Also visible are house foundations, and there are other foundations in nearby fields. The whole site was excavated in the 1930s by British archaeologist Margaret Murray.

After exploring the site, follow the Camí de Trepucó onwards. It rises, then levels out, passing houses and fields. Turn right at a crossroads to follow the Camí Llarg. This narrow road broadens considerably before it reaches a junction with the busy **Me-8 road**. Turn right and cross over the road, as well as crossing a cycleway and footway, to reach the Restaurante El Picadero.

Map continues on page 57

Walk through the restaurant car park and follow a track onwards, with woods on both sides. Turn right at a junction as marked, following the Camí Darrere

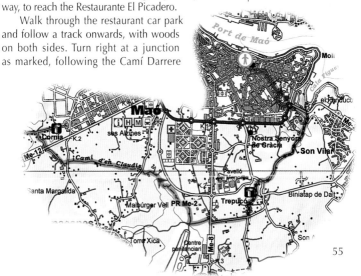

Malbúger Vell through woods, and through a gateway in a drystone wall. The track narrows and swings left, rising and falling, flanked by walls and woods, sometimes worn to bare limestone. Avoid two paths off to the right, which lead to a road by-passing Maó. The path becomes a track, the Camí Vell de Llucmaçanes, in an area of fields dotted with houses.

Cross a road called Camí Baix. Continue straight along a walled path, the **Camí d'en Claudis**, which gradually broadens, becoming a track leading to another road. ◀ Walk straight ahead along a road called Camí des Corb, turning right along a track before reaching the garden centre called Es Bosc. The track joins a road, still called Camí des Corb, passing a fire station to reach the busy **Me-12 road**.

Cross the road and continue along the Camí de Curnia, keeping left at a junction. At the next junction, the PR-IB-Me 2 trail is signposted left, up the Camí Vell de Sant Climent. ◀ However, the Talaiot de Curnia Vell is signposted to the right and is worth a visit. To reach it, follow the Camí de Curnia until the tarmac ends, then turn right, up through a gate.

> There are actually two talaiots at **Talaiot de Curnia Vell**, both of which have been excavated recently. The western one features a huddle of house sites at its base, and very steep stone steps to its top. The eastern one, reached by following a mown grass path, has a corridor through its middle, and stone cisterns for collecting water. The site dates from the 3rd century BC, though ceramics dating from the 13th century were found on the site.

Retrace your steps and follow the Camí Vell de Sant Climent uphill. Cross over the **Me-14 road** and continue as signposted from a mapboard. A patchy tarmac road narrows, then broadens, climbing to a road where there are abundant signposts and aircraft navigation lights. ◀ The PR-IB-Me 1 trail (followed in the first stage of the Coast to Coast walk) is signposted to the right, up

Llucmaçanes lies off-route to the south, visited in Walk 5.

Note the old quarries and square-cut caves.

The airport runway is very close and the passenger terminal is 2km (1¼ miles) distant.

the road called Camí de Torelló, but the PR-IB-Me 2 trail turns left. However, it is worth turning right for a short detour to nearby archaeological sites.

There are two talaiots at Talaiot de Curnia Vell; this is the western one

Detour to Torellonet Vell and Torelló

Keep right at a junction and follow the Camí de Torelló, to find the **Talaiot de Torellonet Vell** on the left. A hands-on scramble leads to the top, where a flashing navigation light has been erected, beside a fine square-cut doorway. There are house sites and cisterns at its base, and there is a tumbled talaiot nearby. Further along the road, a grassy track heads right, signposted for the **Basílica des Fornàs de Torelló**. This site is securely

Map continues on page 59

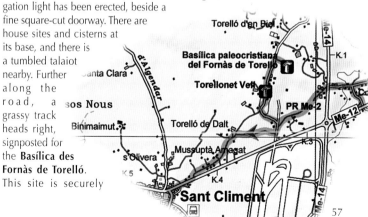

57

The Talaiot de Torellonet Vell is crowned with square-blocked doorway

fenced and covered, protecting an amazing mosaic floor and the ground-plan of an ancient church. Retrace your steps to continue along the PR-IB-Me 2 trail.

Turn left to follow the road, then turn right to follow a track, rising and falling past fields. Join a road and keep left, in effect walking straight ahead and gently down it. Pass houses to join the busy Me-12 road, and turn right to head straight for **Sant Climent** (shops, bars, banks with ATMs, buses). Just on the outskirts of the village, turn left as marked along Camí des Pou des Cards, then turn left along a road leaving the village. However, turn right as marked along Carrer de Sant Miquel. ◀

Note that the village bus stop lies to the right, on Carrer de Sant Climent.

At the end of Carrer de Sant Miquel, on the edge of the village, turn left to follow the Camí de sa Forana. Pass houses and cultivated plots; when the road drops, watch out on the right to spot a modern stone-built *barraca*, or cattle shed, in the shape of a ziggurat. The road rises and falls, crossing a valley called Barranc de ses Vinyes. Walk up the road and keep straight ahead at a junction at **Binixiquer**. Walk straight past rows of detached houses and gardens, passing a signpost and continuing along the narrower Camí de Binicalaf. The road later rises past houses, levelling out beside the boulder walls of the Talaiot de Binicalaf, which lies to the right. ▸

If you climb the talaiot there are views back to Sant Climent and the airport, along a stretch of the south coast and inland to Monte Toro.

Continue along the road and keep straight ahead along a narrower road, which soon ends. Go straight up a track as signposted, undulating past fields and bushes, then pass houses and reach a road at the **Urbanització Calascoves**. Walk straight ahead to a spacious junction, and cross over to find a track signposted for 'Cales Coves' and 'COVES' (nearby bar restaurants; bus stop on the Me-12 road).

Simply follow the track, or dirt road, gently downhill, then a little more steeply, flanked throughout by dense woodland with margins of càrritx. Go through a gateway and keep descending, taking note of the Camí de Cavalls (GR223, Stage 2) as it crosses the track. Keep straight ahead to reach the attractive rocky inlet of **Calascoves**, where an interesting 'necropolis' can be explored. There is a house to the right, and canes grow thickly before a tiny sandy beach is reached. ▸

Although the PR-IB-Me 2 finishes here, there is no transport unless a pick-up can be arranged.

The cliffs to the left are dotted with the **Necrópolis de Calascoves**, hand-hewn caves that were used for burials. The most sensitive of the caves are blocked by sheet-iron coverings, but narrow paths and steep

Map continues on page 61

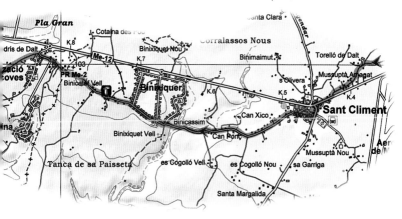

The peculiar bar/ disco clinging to cliffs at Cova d'en Xoroi near Cala en Porter

flights of rock steps can be used to visit some of them. Follow yellow arrows on a blue background to explore.

Either retrace your steps back to the Urbanització Calascoves to catch a bus, or follow the GR223 as signposted left for Cala en Porter. For the latter, climb from the valley using a rugged path as signposted, go through a gap in a drystone wall and follow the wall up through woods. Cross a rise and walk down through a gate. Turn right uphill again and walk through more woods. Drift left from the wall and go down through a gate. A path splits from a track, crosses a dip, then re-joins the track to go through a gap in a wall. Head up to the right as marked, through a gate, and follow the path to go down through another gate. Cross a wooded valley and climb the other side as marked. Go through a gate onto a road with houses alongside.

Turn left along the road, up to a football pitch. Turn right up another road, the Travessera de l'Avinguda Central. This levels out and joins the Avinguda Central where the GR223 turns right. ▶ Follow the road over a rise, across a dip, then over another rise into the centre of **Cala en Porter** (accommodation, supermarkets, ATM, bar restaurants, buses, taxis).

Turning left leads to Cova d'en Xoroi.

The **Cova d'en Xoroi** is now used as a disco and nightclub, but can be entered at other times by curious visitors. The entrance fee includes a 'free' drink at the bar, and the cave is worth visiting simply for its unusual character and exceptional cliff views. According to local lore, Xoroi came from the sea, possibly shipwrecked. He occupied a spacious cave in the cliffs, and kidnapped a young woman. She bore him three sons before anyone discovered them. Xoroi and his eldest son jumped into the sea to their deaths, while the woman and her other two sons were taken inland to Alaior (see **www.covadenxoroi.com**).

61

WALK 8
Es Migjorn Gran and Cova des Coloms

Start/Finish	Es Migjorn Gran
Distance	9km (5½ miles)
Total Ascent/Descent	130m (425ft)
Time	3hrs
Terrain	Mostly easy roads and tracks, with a series of rugged paths in the middle.
Refreshment	Plenty of choice in Es Migjorn Gran, and a bar off-route in the direction of Sant Tomàs.
Public transport	Daily buses serve Es Migjorn Gran from Maó, Alaior and Ciutadella. Summer buses serve nearby Sant Tomàs.

This short walk leaves the village of Es Migjorn Gran and passes through gentle countryside at first. A rugged path descends into the Barranc de Binigaus, where an enormous cave called the Cova des Coloms can be visited. Later, the walk can be extended to the coast and links easily with the resort of Sant Tomàs. In the other direction it links with Stage 3 of the GR223 to Cala Galdana, or the rugged cliff coast of Walk 9.

Start at the bus stop in **Es Migjorn Gran**, on Plaça Menorca (accommodation, shops, bars, restaurants, post office, banks with ATMs, buses, taxis). Follow the road signposted for Ciutadella, the Avinguda Binicudrell, and take the second road on the left, almost on the way out of the village. This is the unsigned Camí de sa Malagarba. As the road levels out, there is parking alongside, and signs indicate the way to a Hotel Rural, Cementiri Municipal and Cova dels Coloms. The road narrows after the old stone farmhouse of Bini Cudrell.

At **Binicodrell** a gate gives access to field on the left, where there are two talaiots. The more substantial of these has a narrow S-shaped path to its top, where there is a good view of Es Migjorn Gran, Monte Toro and the surrounding countryside.

View of Es Migjorn Gran from the top of a talaiot at Bini Cudrell

The road is flanked by an avenue of pines as it runs gently downhill. Keep right to pass a cemetery, then the road rises gently. ▶ Pass the farm of Sa Vinya des Metge Camps and keep following the road gently downhill. Reach a tidy arrangement of buildings lying to the right, which forms the Hotel Rural Binigaus Vell.

Note another talaiot on the right, which has no access.

Follow a track ahead, signposted 'Cuevas/Caves'. This rises a short way, then descends. When it levels out, there is a sign on the left, along with a well-trodden path. Turn left along the path; the route returns via the track. The path is wonderfully level and even at first, but as it drops down through woods it becomes very uneven. When there are views, limestone cliffs are seen rearing up in most directions. The path finally reaches the bed of the **Barranc de Binigaus**, where there is a junction.

Keep left and climb, turning left up a zigzag stone-buttressed path on a cliff. The path leads to a cave of enormous size, the **Cova des Coloms**. ▶ Once explored, retrace your steps back to the path junction, then continue down through the valley.

A torch is only required to explore the furthest recesses of the cave.

The path is easy, even when it wriggles past a couple of huge boulders. It is well-trodden, and once it settles

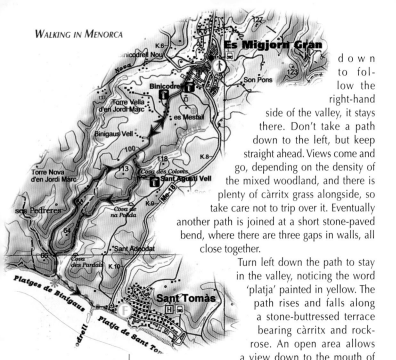

down to follow the right-hand side of the valley, it stays there. Don't take a path down to the left, but keep straight ahead. Views come and go, depending on the density of the mixed woodland, and there is plenty of càrritx grass alongside, so take care not to trip over it. Eventually another path is joined at a short stone-paved bend, where there are three gaps in walls, all close together.

Turn left down the path to stay in the valley, noticing the word 'platja' painted in yellow. The path rises and falls along a stone-buttressed terrace bearing càrritx and rock-rose. An open area allows a view down to the mouth of the valley, framing the sea. The path suddenly drops onto a track, where a sign points back to the Cova des Coloms. When stone water troughs are reached there are a number of choices.

To reach Sant Tomàs – 1.5km (1 mile) off-route

Follow the track straight towards the sea, with a slope of pines to the right and fields to the left. At a junction, where there is a shelter to the right, turn left and cross the soft sandy beach at the **Platges de Binigaus**. Continue along the low cliff coast, and pass a curious structure, which is an entrance to a Civil War bunker, with rifle-holes pointing across the path. The well-trodden path overlooks limestone slab islets, then passes seawards of the Bar Es Bruc. A road runs inland, flanked by pines, and there is a Camí de Cavalls mapboard nearby. The resort of **Sant Tomàs** lies ahead, served by road and coastal path (accommodation, shops, bars, restaurants, summer buses).

To reach Cala Galdana – 9km (5½ miles) off-route
Follow the track straight towards the sea, with a slope of pines to the right and fields to the left. At a junction, where there is a shelter to the right, turn right as marked by an arrow for Cala Escorxada and follow Walk 9 in reverse.

To return to Es Migjorn Gran, turn right along the track, leaving the water troughs, and keep straight ahead, ignoring the GR223, which climbs to the

A track leads to a sandy beach at Platges de Binigaus

left. ▶ The track runs through a wooded valley, and a couple of sweeping bends later climbs high above it, passing a cliff where there is a well and a cattle trough. There are gates ahead, so turn left along a narrow path, passing left of a big, stout old house.

This offers another route to Cala Galdana; see GR223 Stage 3.

The path rejoins the track and continues climbing, with walls on both sides. Walk up to a well, troughs and gates. A sign on the right indicates a path down to Platja de Binigaus, but keep walking ahead, gently down the track. This rises and falls, then passes the path used for the rugged descent earlier in the day. Continue along the track, joining the road near the Hotel Rural Binigaus Vell, and head straight back to **Es Migjorn Gran**.

WALK 9
Cala Galdana and Sant Tomàs

Start	Cala Galdana
Finish	Sant Tomàs
Distance	12km (7½ miles)
Total Ascent/Descent	300m (985ft)
Time	4hrs
Terrain	Apart from a few easy woodland tracks, mostly rugged coastal cliff paths with a few short ascents and descents.
Refreshment	Plenty of choice at Cala Galdana and Sant Tomàs.
Public transport	Summer buses serve Cala Galdana and Sant Tomàs.

A splendid cliff coast path runs between the little resorts of Cala Galdana and Sant Tomàs. There are several rocky coves along the way, with white sand beaches. There are no habitations near the coast, and the inland parts are often well-wooded. Although this route is described as a one-way trip, it can be made into a circuit by returning along the Camí de Cavalls, or GR223. This wanders far inland before returning to the coast near Cala Galdana.

Start in the resort of **Cala Galdana**, at the mouth of a tidal river, where a footbridge leads to El Mirador Bar Restaurante on a limestone islet. Cross the footbridge, but instead of walking to the restaurant, turn left to walk along a sandy beach, towards the Sol Gavilanes. Turn left inland just

Map continues on page 68

The sandy bay of Cala Mitjana, outside the resort of Cala Galdana

before the hotel, walking up a valley shaded by holm oaks. This is part of the Camí de Cavalls, or GR223, so watch for signposts and markers, and turn right to climb from the valley to a road junction. Turn right to follow the road, Avinguda de sa Punta, above the Sol Gavilanes. Turn left along the short Carrer Camí des Cavalls, which ends in a turning circle. ▶

It is worth walking to the end of the Avinguda de sa Punta, where a fine viewpoint overlooks Cala Galdana.

Walk off the end of Carrer Camí des Cavalls, pass a mapboard, go through a gateway and turn left. A path follows a stone wall down through woods, rising a little, then heading right along a fenced rock lip. The path rises and broadens, with a limekiln on the right. Turn left at a junction (right is for a viewpoint only) then turn right down a broad track, and keep right, passing a rock lip where there is a cave house. Walk down to a rocky bay where there are old quarries, and note square-cut stone blocks that were piled up but never removed. ▶

A notice explains about these quarries.

Walk up and down a track cut from the bedrock, with good views of the coast when the trees allow. Turn right down a flight of wooden steps, cross the sandy beach at **Cala Mitjana**, and climb stone steps and cut rock steps, marked by an arrow and a signpost. The steps later give

There is a Civil War bunker to the right and a view of the coast.

way to an easy forest path. Go through a gap in a wall and follow the arrow to the left. ◄

Follow a very clear and gentle path, and watch for a ruined hut and limekiln to the right. Further along an undulating track there is another limekiln on the right. Go through a gateway gap in a wall and descend gently through another gap. An open grassy clearing features a cairn shelter just off-route at **s'Arenal**, otherwise follow the path gently up into woods. Although narrower, the path is well-trodden, but becomes more rugged as the descent steepens. A final set of rock steps leads down to a beach flanked by cliffs at **Cala Trebalúger**. There is a river here that has to be crossed, either by jumping from a rocky edge, or by walking through a curious cave/tunnel, then wading across.

After crossing the sandy beach, come ashore onto rocks and look for marker posts bearing arrows. These reveal a path climbing steeply on a slope of pines, scrub woodland, heather and rock-rose to **Marina de Trebalúger**. Rock steps have been cut at the top, then the path runs easily through a gateway in a wall. Walk down-hill, the slope steep and rocky on some short stretches. Emerge on rugged, crumbling coarse-textured rock above an inlet with a sea cave at its head. Very little grows here, except for a few tufts of vegetation, though dense wood-lands rise inland.

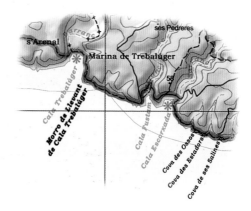

Map continues on page 70

The path is marked by posts and later climbs back into the woods. Reach a bend on a vehicle track, but turn right down a rugged path. ▶ Walk towards a sand and seaweed beach at the head of a rocky cove at **Cala Fustam**. Climb inland to a gate on the track, and turn right to follow the track up through the woods. It soon runs down to another sandy beach in a rocky cove at **Cala Escorxada**, where there is a Civil War bunker.

A safety fence guards against a sudden drop into a chasm and the sea.

Either follow a rope-flanked path across dunes, or go onto the sandy beach, then climb from it. The path runs in and out of woods, climbs stone steps, enjoys fine views and has some fenced-off cliff edges. After turning round a point, the path runs through woods, then it goes down and up stone steps above the very rocky **Cova des Ossos**. After a stretch through woods, the path runs down along the cliff coast, passing an inlet with a sea cave at its head, before rising through a gap in a wall. The path reaches a rocky edge. ▶ Some stretches of the path have fencing alongside. Pass an inlet where the sea often makes a gurgling sound; the path then heads inland, up through dense woods, but still runs parallel to the coast. The path

Here the resorts of Sant Tomàs and Son Bou come into view ahead.

The cliff coast path features fenced sections on the way to Platges de Binigaus

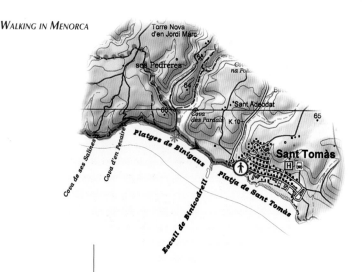

By turning left at a shelter and following a track, Stage 3 of the GR223 can be followed back to Cala Galdana.

broadens and descends among tall pines, then narrows and undulates, before becoming broad and stony as it drops to the sandy **Platges de Binigaus**. ◀

Cross the soft sandy beach and continue along the low cliff coast. Pass a curious structure, an entrance to a Civil War bunker, with rifle-holes pointing across the path. The well-trodden path overlooks limestone slab islets, then passes seawards of the Bar Es Bruc. A road runs inland, flanked by pines, and there is a Camí de Cavalls mapboard nearby. The resort of **Sant Tomàs** lies ahead, served by road and coastal path (accommodation, shops, bars, restaurants, summer buses).

WALK 10

Ferreries and Cova des Moro

Start/Finish	Snack Bar Vimpi, Ferreries
Distance	12km (7½ miles) there and back or 14km (8¾ miles) with the variant
Total Ascent/Descent	200 or 360m (655 or 1180ft)
Time	3hrs 30min or 4hrs 30min
Terrain	For a there-and-back walk, the route is all along easy roads and tracks. The variant return involves steeper tracks and field paths.
Refreshment	Plenty of choice in Ferreries.
Public transport	Regular daily buses serve Ferreries from Maó and Ciutadella.

Cova des Moro is an interesting archaeological site that can be reached quite easily by following farm roads and tracks from Ferreries. Most walkers who go there return the same way. However, there are impressive views across the Barranc de sa Cova, which is flanked by limestone cliffs, and some may wish to explore further. There is a way through this valley that walkers occasionally use, but it relies on the goodwill of local farmers. However, if the low-lying fields are ploughed, one stretch will prove difficult to follow.

Start from the bus stop at the Snack Bar Vimpi in **Ferreries**, and walk round the corner and down a road past the post office (*Correos*). Turn right at the bottom, along the Avinguda Son Morera, parallel to a river in a concrete channel. The road joins the Me-20 road on the edge of town. Turn left to follow the road over a bridge spanning the river. Later, turn right up a road signposted for Son Mercer de Baix and Cova des Moro.

A concrete road climbs through a cutting in red sandstone, then a broad gravel track rises across a slope of pines, holm oaks and limestone, which climbs and bends left a couple of times. ▶ Go up through a wood and out into fields, passing a row of upended limestone blocks, one of which is set in a concrete base near **Son Mercer de**

There are good views of Ferreries.

A barraca, or stone cattle shed, between Son Mercer de Dalt and Son Mercer de Baix

Another small barraca lies to the left.

Dalt. A sign points downhill to the right, for Poblat Son Mercer de Baix. Someone has scratched 'don't go' on the sign, but that is where we will be heading anyway!

Simply follow the clearest and most well-used track down between fields, avoiding all other tracks. There is a building up to the right, and later a distinctive *barraca*, a stone-built cattle shed, to the right. Pass a gateway marked 'Son Merce de Baix' and cross a gentle rise. ◄ Go through the farmyard at **Son Mercer de Baix**, following two signposts and continuing down a track. Note a third signpost, where tracks part, and keep right to cross a dip. Rise and undulate through a bushy and grassy area, then head generally downhill. A signpost on the left points up a grassy path, through a gateway, where there is a noticeboard explaining about Cova des Moro.

The main feature of **Cova des Moro** is a 'naviform', or upturned boat-like building, probably dating from around 1300BC. A surprisingly spacious room is supported on three columns, while further uphill are the low ruins of other buildings and structures. At the very top of the site there is an amazing view of the Barranc de sa Cova, with its limestone cliffs, fields and orchards.

Walk back along the undulating track, back across the dip and uphill. When a signpost is reached near **Son Mercer de Baix**, either continue retracing the outward route back to Ferreries, or turn sharp right, down through a gate, following another track for a different way back. The track crosses a dip and rises, with cattle troughs and a long stone cattle shed to the left. Keep climbing straight up past fields, then wind down a slope of trees, bushy scrub and càrritx, where the track has been cut into the limestone cliffs. After some hairpin bends the track continues gently up through the **Barranc de sa Cova** towards a farmhouse.

The valley floor is planted as an orchard; when the houses are reached at **Son Fideu**, fork right down a grassy track, and right again down steps. Walk round the head of the orchard and go through a gate. Turn sharp left, doubling back along a short track towards the houses, but before reaching them, go through a gateway gap in a wall to enter a field. Keep to the left-hand side of the field, which has a brambly edge, in the valley of the **Torrent de Son Gras**. ▶ It will be grassy, mown or ploughed. If ploughed, then it will be difficult underfoot.

There are cliffs on both sides of the valley.

At the end of the field a grassy track rises, which quickly becomes cut into the rock wall of the valley. The track winds higher and higher, passing areas of woodland, bushy scrub and càrritx. Go through a gateway and the track levels out; notice a barraca in a field to the left. Follow the track straight ahead and down into a field. This field could be grassy, mown or ploughed, but the likelihood is that tractor wheel ruts will run around the left-hand side, so walk that way. ▶ Swing right at the corner and climb, joining a clearer walled track. Turn left down

There are short-lived views of Son Mercer de Baix, a cattle shed and Son Mercer de Dalt.

73

Son Mercer de Dalt is passed again on the return to Ferreries.

it, then follow it up to a junction, rejoining a well-used track followed earlier in the day.

Turn right up towards **Son Mercer de Dalt**, then walk down the bendy track with views of Ferreries, and continue down the concrete track to the main Me-20 road. Turn left to follow the road over the bridge, and turn right back into **Ferreries** (see end of Coast to Coast Stage 3 for an extension to visit the Ermita de Ferreries). To vary the last part, turn left to pass a sports pitch and reach the Centre de la Natura de Menorca. Head slightly right after it on the triangular Plaça Menorca. Follow Carrer Pau Pons straight to the Plaça Espanya, then turn right to follow the Avinguda Verge del Toro to the roundabout and bus stop at the Snack Bar Vimpi.

WALK 11
Cala Macarella and Cala Turqueta

Start/Finish	Cala Macarella
Alternative Start/Finish	Cala Turqueta
Distance	8km (5 miles)
Total Ascent/Descent	250m (820ft)
Time	3hrs
Terrain	An intricate network of tracks and paths, sometimes in woods and sometimes along the coastal cliffs.
Refreshment	Plenty of choice at Cala Galdana. Café at Cala Macarella.
Public transport	None to Cala Macarella or Cala Turqueta, but nearby Cala Galdana has summer bus services.
Access	There is road access from Ciutadella, signposted first for 'Platges Costa Sud'. Later, a junction is reached at Son Vivó, where a left turn is signposted for the beaches of Macarelleta, Macarella and Turqueta. When the chapel called Ermita Sant Joan de Missa is reached, either keep straight ahead for Turqueta, or go right for Macarella. Whichever is chosen as the starting point, continue all the way to the road-end car parks.

Walkers who follow the Camí de Cavalls, or GR223, west of Cala Galdana, soon reach Cala Macarella. The route then heads inland before returning to the coast at Cala Turqueta. However, a fine cliff coast path is also available, and this is described below. Motorists can drive from Cuitadella to road-end car parks above both Cala Macarella and Cala Turqueta. It is also possible to approach this walk from Cala Galdana, which has summer bus services, by following the GR223 Stage 4, which adds only a little extra distance.

From the large **car park** above Cala Macarella follow a gravel track beyond the car park and a notice saying it is 15min to the beach. The track has a rope to the left and a wall to the right. Turn right along a path, descending with ropes on both sides. The gravel path winds down a slope that is densely wooded at times. Pass above a café on the

The sandy beach at Cala Macarella is surrounded by pine trees

The beach can also be reached by following Stage 4 of the GR223 for 3.5km (2 miles) from Cala Galdana.

slope or, if it is open, perhaps take a short-cut to it for refreshment. The path links with a flight of wooden steps leading down to the beach at **Cala Macarella**. ◄

Walk across the sandy beach and climb up a rocky slope of pines and bushes to reach a signpost. The GR223 heads right, but turn left as marked by an arrow to follow a cliff-path instead. The path is rocky as it climbs, with fine views of the bay. There are steep stone steps with fencing alongside, more steps later and a rocky point is turned before the path descends more steps and winds down to a little sandy beach hemmed in by cliffs at **Cala Macarelleta**.

Walk across the sandy beach and pick up a path rising between ropes into a valley of pines, quickly reaching a GR223 signpost. Turn left up a narrow unmarked path, quickly climbing a flight of stone steps. A steep, rough and rocky path reaches a junction near a cliff edge. ◄

Turn left for a short there-and-back path to a fine viewpoint looking back into the coves.

Turn right to follow the well-wooded path, at first without views of the cliffs, but when bushy scrub develops later, the cliffs can be seen near **Punta de na Gall**, and maybe distant Mallorca can be glimpsed.

A path heads to the right, inland, but keep straight ahead. Later, when a wall appears at **Penyes d'Alparico**, go

through a
gateway gap.

The path is marked by posts
bearing arrows, running gently down past a few arbutus
trees, then gently uphill. Watch for a GR223 signpost
to the right, at a complex junction, but keep left along
a narrowing path through scrub, returning to the cliffs
and following them round into a fine rock-bound cove.
Eventually drop to a sandy beach beside a large palm tree
at **Cala Turqueta**. Walk to the head of the beach, then
inland a little, and quickly turn right to follow the broad
path marked and signposted for Cala Macarella, via the
GR233.

Alternative start from Cala Turqueta

The road from Sant Joan de Missa becomes a track signposted for Turqueta. Leave the **car park** and follow a
track that is walled at first, through woods containing
pines and holm oaks. The track is bendy as it descends
in a shallow wooded valley with rock outcrops and
cliffs on both sides. Walk through a walled enclosure
to find mapboards and noticeboards at the head of the
sandy beach at **Cala Turqueta**. To continue, turn left to
follow the GR223 as marked and signposted to Cala
Macarella.

The sandy beach at Cala Turqueta, flanked by low cliffs and pine trees

Cala Macarelleta is only a short distance straight ahead.

The GR223 climbs through woods, goes through a gateway gap in a wall and reaches a complex junction. Keep left and follow a lumpy path through an area of scrub, through a wall, and keep walking onwards among pines on **Marina d'Alparica**. Turn right at a signpost and walk gently down a broad path, then descend more steeply through pine forest in a valley, with a cliff along the right-hand side. Level out at a junction and signpost passed earlier in the day. ◄ Turn left up a broad sandy path, which narrows and passes beneath a cliff. Follow the path down and up a bit, continuing up a buttressed path. Go through a gateway in a wall and drift right.

Alternative finish at Cala Turqueta
Turn back right at a signposted path junction to follow the cliff path back to Cala Turqueta along the coast.

Turn left at a signposted path junction, then right at another junction. The path descends and steepens on a densely-wooded sloped, going down a few log steps to return to **Cala Macarella**. Finish by walking straight inland to reach the car park.

WALK 12
Sant Joan, Son Saura and Son Catlar

Start/Finish	Ermita Sant Joan de Missa
Distance	20km (12½ miles)
Total Ascent/Descent	100m (330ft)
Time	5hrs
Terrain	Mostly along roads at gentle gradients, with a more rugged, wooded coastal path in the middle.
Refreshment	None.
Public transport	None.

This part of Menorca lacks bus services; access is from Ciutadella, and long stretches of road-walking are required to complete this circuit. However, the countryside is pleasant and the white sand beaches of Cala Turqueta and Platges de Son Saura are very attractive. Historical interest includes a fine countryside chapel, old farmhouses, Civil War defences and the splendid archaeological site of Poblat de Son Catlar.

From Ciutadella follow a road signposted for 'Sant Joan de Missa' and 'Platges Costa Sud'. When a road junction is reached at Son Vivó, turn left to follow the road to the attractive countryside chapel called the **Ermita Sant Joan de Missa**. Park tidily here and continue on foot along the narrow road signposted for Turqueta. This soon reaches a junction at Son Foch; keep right and walk at gentle gradients past fields. There are woodlands around **Son Vecete**, which lies to the right, and livestock may be present around **Marjal Vella** later.

The road runs into a wood, then turn right down a track signposted for Turqueta, undulating on the way to a car park. Leave the car park and follow a track that is walled at first, through woods containing pines and holm oaks. The track is bendy as it descends in a shallow wooded valley with rock outcrops and cliffs on both sides. Walk through a walled enclosure to find map-

*This circular walk
starts and finishes at
the Ermita Sant Joan
de Missa*

This is also followed
on Stage 4 of the
GR223.

There are views
inland to Monte Toro,
and ahead to distant
Mallorca.

boards and noticeboards at the head of the sandy beach
at **Cala Turqueta**.

Turn right to follow a signposted and waymarked
coastal path. ◄ A path follows a wall up a wooded slope
with no views. Go through a gate in a wall and continue
through woods. Go down and cross a path that offers
access to the coast, but keep ahead and climb instead.
There are some short but sometimes steep and rocky
ascents and descents, through bushy scrub to pass the
mouth of the bay. ◄

Cross a lumpy and awkward rocky platform at **Punta des Tambors**, where vegetation is short and sits in little hollows. Head back into the scrub on the way round the next bay, reaching a signpost. Turn left along a path that falls and rises, over and over. Turn right to reach a

Pine trees lean over a dirt road heading inland from Platges de Son Saura

mapboard near **Cala des Talaier**. Turn left to visit the sandy beach flanked by low cliffs.

Climb past the mapboard and turn left at a signpost, following a path through a little gate and out of the scrub onto a rocky platform. Turn round the headland of **Punta des Governador**. ◄ An area of pine forest is roped off from the rocky coast. The ropes, pines and rock all meet the sandy beach of **Platges de Son Saura** at a signpost.

Note trenches cut into the rock and underground structures, all associated with the Civil War.

Walk along the beach, avoiding any deep piles of seaweed. A line of sand dunes are roped off, and at the far side of the bay a footbridge spans another rock trench.

Turn left along a track and follow it round a low, rocky point covered in scrub woodland. Reach another sand and seaweed beach called Platja des Banyul. Watch for a gap and walk inland, following a track to a large car park. Follow the road inland, passing several fields, and later note a *barraca*, or stone-built cattle shed, to the right. The outer surface resembles a huge untidy cairn, but the inside surface is a perfect dome shape. ▸ Also note the castle-like house of **Torre Saura Vella** far away to the left. Follow the road onwards past more fields, to find a small car park on the right, where there is access to the archaeological site of **Son Catlar**.

There are many more of these barracas dotted around the fields.

Go through a gate and follow a grassy path to **Son Catlar**, a well-defended Bronze Age village site, which remained in use during the Roman occupation. There are notices available, mapping out 20 main features of interest, starting with a burial chamber, and suggesting an anti-clockwise circuit around the exterior of the site, followed by an anti-clockwise circuit of the interior. The exterior is protected by an impressive 'Cyclopean' wall, incorporating two entrance portals, five towers and three bastions. The interior contains four *talaiots*, a *taula* enclosure where the taula lacks a cap-stone, house sites, hypostyle chamber, animal corrals and structures assumed to be sentry boxes.

Continue along the road, walking at gentle gradients across **Planet Vermell**, past more fields. Later, notice a huddle of buildings to the right at **Santa Rosa**. A road junction is reached soon afterwards, near the big building of **Son Vivó**. Turn right to follow the road back to the **Ermita Sant Joan de Missa**.

WALK 13
Santa Àgueda and Cala del Pilar

Start	Santa Àgueda
Finish	Alzinar de Dalt
Distance	11km (6½ miles)
Total Ascent	350m (1150ft)
Total Descent	400m (1310ft)
Time	3hrs
Terrain	An easy hill climb, followed by easy, undulating roads and tracks, linked by a more rugged coastal path.
Refreshment	None.
Public transport	None. Arrange a taxi drop-off and pick-up from Ferreries.

This walk visits a splendid hill-top fort, Castell de Santa Àgueda, and two north-coast beaches. Access is difficult, as there are no buses, and buses between Maó and Ciutadella will not stop on the busy Me-1 road, where the Camí des Alocs and Camí del Pilar head northwards. Nor are cars much use, unless one can be parked at either end of the route. The easiest access is by taxi from Ferreries; be sure to negotiate a pick-up for later from the finish, where there may not be mobile phone coverage.

Hire a taxi to travel along the minor road of **Camí des Alocs**, asking to be dropped near Castell de Santa Àgueda. The starting point for the walk is a junction between this road, the access road for the farm of Santa Cecilia and the track up to the castle. There is a signpost and gate, and the track is flanked by trees and bushes as it climbs. It becomes quite well-wooded once it passes into holm oaks and pines. Sudden right and left bends can be short-cut using a stone-paved path, but this ends with a bit of an awkward scramble back onto the track.

The track reaches a grassy shoulder, then another stone-paved stretch can be followed, passing a ruined

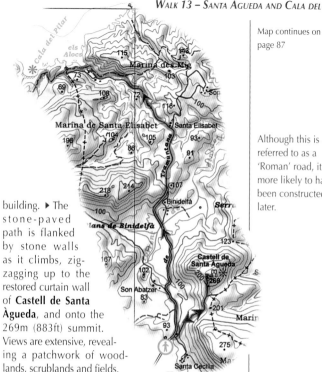

Map continues on page 87

Although this is referred to as a 'Roman' road, it is more likely to have been constructed later.

building. ▶ The stone-paved path is flanked by stone walls as it climbs, zig-zagging up to the restored curtain wall of **Castell de Santa Àgueda**, and onto the 269m (883ft) summit. Views are extensive, revealing a patchwork of woodlands, scrublands and fields.

There is evidence to suggest that the hill-top **Castell de Santa Àgueda** was occupied before the Roman conquest, but the walls surrounding the summit were constructed by Moorish occupiers, with different phases at different times. The impressive entrance to the Castell, and the enclosure beyond, appear to have been built at the same time, with 11th-century round towers and 12th-century square towers. A further enclosure was added in the 13th century. The site was known as Sen Agaiz, but following the displacement of the Moors in 1287 it was renamed Santa Àgueda, and

The fortified gateway to the hilltop Castell de Santa Àgueda

a church was built. The site had been abandoned by 1343.

Walk back down to the road junction and turn right to follow the road through the countryside, noting the access to **Son Abatzer** up to the left. Walk down the road into a dip, then rise again. Cross another dip, where green fields turn red when ploughed. Walk up the road, passing above the farm of **Binidelfà**. Go through a cutting in red sandstone and walk down a track into a forest. Cross a broad dip full of bushes and scrub woodland, and continue towards a white house called **Santa Elisabet**.

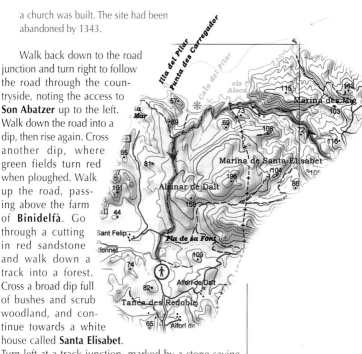

Turn left at a track junction, marked by a stone saying 'P 2KM'. Go down the winding track, eventually forking right and reaching a little house, where mapboards and the pebbly beach of **els Alocs** lies just beyond. ▸

A ceramic plaque reading 'Camí des Cavalls' is mounted on a rock.

Turn left to climb onto a headland, where a fence runs alongside. Follow markers for the GR223, looking back to els Alocs, then down to another small bouldery beach, often covered in driftwood. The stony path descends and climbs through bushes, then drops steeply with the aid of log steps. Pass a signpost on sandstone slabs and note that a path on the right is prohibited, due to a landslide. Go down a rock step and cross a small pebbly beach. Watch carefully while climbing a rocky edge to spot a geological 'unconformity' where two different beds of sandstone join at the 'wrong' angle.

Soft red sandstone, wooden steps and a golden beach at Cala del Pilar

Follow a path up a rocky and stony slope for a view of **Cala del Pilar** and its golden beach. Stay on the path as marked through bushy scrub, and if a visit to the beach is required, use a flight of wooden steps on a crumbling red slope from a prominent notice-board, and return the same way to continue. The path is often sandy as it climbs, though firmer when it crosses stony or rocky areas. Watch for markers, as there is a maze of unmarked paths on the slope. A stretch of fencing on the right offers a view over a cliff, where there are a couple of old cave houses. Eventually, the path levels out among pines.

Turn left to follow a path through a broad gap in a wall. The path rises and falls as it runs through pine forest dotted with holm oaks. There is a wall to the right for a while, then it is lost to view. When the wall is seen again, the track rises through a gap in it, and then soon settles down for a gentle descent through woods at **Alzinar de Dalt**, mostly sandy underfoot, though sometimes worn to bedrock. When the track splits go either way, as both stretches rejoin. Walk down to a huge holm oak tree and a gate at Alzinar. An access track for Son Felip runs off-route to the right, but turn left to enter a large **car park**. ◄

This is where a pick-up needs to be organised in advance, as there may not be mobile phone coverage.

Handwritten annotations at top: "10.30", "12-40", "return 16.00", "13.25 17.00", "£3.25"

WALK 14
Fornells and Cala Tirant

Start/Finish	Harbour, Fornells
Distance	10km (6¼ miles)
Total Ascent/Descent	110m (360ft)
Time	3hrs
Terrain	Easy road-walking for the first half, then rugged coastal and cliff walking for the second half.
Refreshment	Bars and restaurants at Fornells, Ses Salines and Cala Tirant.
Public transport	Daily buses link Fornells and Ses Salines, with summer buses serving Cala Tirant.

The villages of Fornells and Cala Tirant sit on a rocky peninsula that is just the right size to offer a short day's walk. Although roads are followed between the villages, the rest of the walk features increasingly attractive cliffs and coves, leading to the very rugged and scenic Cap de Fornells. The headland overlooks the narrow channel serving the sheltered waters of Port de Fornells, so it is no surprise to find a prominent castle, tower and other defensive structures.

Start beside the attractive harbour in the village of **Fornells** and follow the broad pavement beside it, which becomes a broad, palm-fringed promenade leading to the edge of the village. Step inland a short way to follow the main road onwards. The pavement runs between the road and a cycleway. ▸ Pass the little resort of **Ses Salines** (accommodation, bars, restaurants, bus services).

There are good views of the sheltered inlet of Port de Fornells, with Monte Toro rising inland.

Turn right to follow a road through an arch announcing 'Platges de Fornells'. Walk up the road, which is also part of the GR223 or Camí de Cavalls, with pines on both sides. At the top there is a view of a fine house to the right, **Tirant Nou**. Follow the road downhill, and on the right at Es Antigons, note an extensive plantation of dragon trees. Go through a roundabout and turn left along Carrer de Baix, into the resort of **Cala Tirant**. ▸

The Camí de Cavalls turns left down a short road to a sandy beach.

Continue along the road from a bus stop, up Carrer de Baix, over a rise and downhill. A left turn is a dead-end, but leads to the Bar Restaurante Reclau. Keep right and walk uphill along Carrer de s'Alcor, where Sa Dolça Cafeteria lies to the left. Walk downhill, then left, where there is a walking sign for Fornells. Continue along Carrer de Dalt, and keep straight ahead as it becomes Carrer Maremar, before swinging left down to a rocky coast to become Carrer de Tamarells. There is a small, rocky cove with jutting crumbling edges of soft sandstone, which is fenced for safety. ◄

There is a view across to the lighthouse on Cap de Cavalleria.

Double back sharp right, signposted for Fornells, following a track round the cove and in front of the last houses in **Platges de Fornells**. Continue along a narrow path, barely trodden, across rocky slopes. The calcareous sandstone contains angular fragments of older rock, making it very rough-textured. Watch carefully for the path: don't go too near the sea, nor too high inland. In the space of a couple of paces, the rock changes from sandstone to an older, contorted, banded and veined rock. Step back onto the calcareous sandstone, then onto the older rock again, and go through a gap in a wall.

The attractive harbour at Fornells overlooks Port de Fornells

Reach a rocky cove and note how the old rock layers are vertical, while just across the cove they are almost horizontal. ▸ Climb from the cove, and the old bedrock is almost vertical again. Step back onto the rugged calcareous sandstone and go through a gap in a wall. Watch for the path splitting to pass either side of a pile of building rubble, with a well-trodden path climbing right, and a less-trodden path heading left. Left is to be preferred, along the foot of the rubble, then there is a short steep climb to go through a gate in a wall at the top. ▸

Continue along the cliff path, with Fornells down to the right and a distinctive tower ahead. Stay on paths close to the cliff edge, avoiding others heading inland, criss-crossing each other. Walk onto the rocky points of **Punta Mala** and especially **Cap de Fornells**, enjoying fine views of cliffs, coves and a rocky islet. Double back and climb to the Torre de Fornells, whose top half is evidently much younger than its bottom half. ▸

Walk down the brick-paved path serving the tower, and a short path to the right is signposted for a grotto, the Ermita de Lourdes. Walk down to a road and follow it back into the village, using a narrow path alongside

If a little stream is flowing, note the curious course the water has to take between the rock beds to the sea.

A cemetery lies to the right, and there is immediate access to the village of Fornells if required.

The tower is generally open in the summer.

91

The Torre de Fornells stands on a rugged limestone headland

that passes derelict structures formerly associated with defence. Join and follow a broad brick-paved path, passing the restored Castell de Sant Antoni, and so return to the harbour in **Fornells** (accommodation, bar restaurants, shops, post office, banks with ATMs, buses, taxis).

WALK 15
Es Grau and Sa Torreta

Start/Finish	Es Grau
Distance	13km (8 miles)
Total Ascent/Descent	250m (820ft)
Time	4hrs
Terrain	Fairly easy coastal paths and farm tracks, and low-lying hills.
Refreshment	Bar restaurants at Es Grau.
Public transport	Summer buses serve Es Grau, otherwise taxi from Maó.

A short and scenic stretch of the GR223, or Camí de Cavalls, can be followed from Es Grau to Cala des Tamarells. From there, a short loop along farm tracks leads to a small and interesting talaiotic site beside the farm of sa Torre Blanca. Although the GR223 is then followed back to Es Grau, the final part can be varied to reach the village. It is possible to link this walk with nearby nature trails at s'Albufera des Grau, explored on Walk 16, though there is a 4km (2½ miles) road-walk between them.

Leave the little coastal village of **Es Grau** by following the Me-5 road back inland. Follow the green tarmac pedestrian strip beside the road, reaching a gate, mapboard and signpost for the GR223 all on the right. Go through the gate and cross a concrete bridge over water. ▶ Either follow the waymarked GR223, or vary it by turning left along the nature trail marked as 'Itinerari 3 Sa Gola'. The GR223 follows a gravel path through tall pine forest, while the nature trail, only slightly longer, follows an interesting boardwalk across marshes, and includes a spur onto a rocky hump overlooking the lagoon of **s'Albufera des Grau**. Both routes join later.

Continue along the path, which passes information boards, a well and cattle troughs, becoming sandy and passing through bushes to reach a sandy beach at **Platja des Grau**. Keep left and follow a rocky and stony path up from the beach, flanked by mixed scrub containing lentisc, spurge, càrritx and cistus. Walk over a crest, down

There is a distant view of Monte Toro.

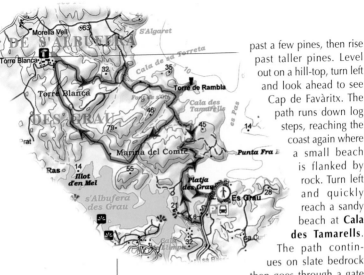

past a few pines, then rise past taller pines. Level out on a hill-top, turn left and look ahead to see Cap de Favàritx. The path runs down log steps, reaching the coast again where a small beach is flanked by rock. Turn left and quickly reach a sandy beach at **Cala des Tamarells**. The path continues on slate bedrock then goes through a gate in a wall. Walk down a sandy path to a track and a signpost. ◀

The GR223 continues towards Cap de Favàritx.

Turn left up the track, which is flanked by bushy scrub, then follow it down through a gate and cross a

A boardwalk nature trail runs across marshy ground near s'Albufera des Grau

94

tiny stream. Rising again, it crosses a gap, then runs down beside a wall. Note a well and trough to the left, then go down through a field. Note another well and trough to the left on the way into another field. There is a view of s'Albufera des Grau to the left, then the grassy track swings right, up past a building, passing from field to field. Cross a gap between wooded hills on **Marina del Comte**. Walk through a grassy dip, continuing up, down and up a wooded slope, where the bedrock is sandstone, levelling out in a field.

Walk through fields and go between white-painted gateposts in a wall. The track crosses a slight limestone rise, passes through a gate, then turns left towards the farm of **sa Torre Blanca**. Go through a gate onto a track beside the farm, but turn right to walk away from the buildings. Turn left through another gate and walk along a track back towards the buildings. ▶ Watch carefully on the right, just before reaching the first building, where there might be a little *taula* sign.

Note an old *era*, or circular threshing floor, to the left.

A small talaiotic site at **Sa Torreta** lies in an enclosure, close to the farm buildings, and the path runs through three gaps in walls to reach it. There is a *talaiot* offering fine views that encompass everything from the nearby coast to Monte Toro. A fine taula is flanked by other stone structures, and there is also a house site.

Walk back along the farm track, through the gate, and walk straight ahead gently downhill. ▶ The descent is well wooded, and limestone gives way to sandstone on the way. Continue down through fields, swing right uphill a little, then go down through a gate to reach a GR223 signpost beside a beach that may be covered in seaweed at **Cala de sa Torreta**. Turn right, noting a little white hut to the left.

Note a fine spreading holm oak tree to the right.

Cross streams flowing into the sea to reach a track and a signpost. Follow the track through pine forest, then turn left out of the forest and climb past a solitary white house. ▶ Follow the path over a rise and down to the next

All the rock around here is old, but there is a thin layer of much younger limestone on top of it.

The small talaiotic site of Sa Torreta stands by the farm of sa Torre Blanca

Visit it if you wish, but the headland is very rocky and the tower itself is badly eroded and in danger of collapsing (see photo in GR223 Stage 10).

little bay. Join a track and turn left to follow it, rising and falling. Note the **Torre de Rambla** off to the left. ◄ The track runs inland, rising gently to reach a few pines and a signpost. Turn left up a sandy path, go through a gate in a wall, then walk down to a little beach flanked by rock at **Cala de Tamarells**.

From here, either retrace the outward route back to the start point, or vary the final stretch by walking along the sandy beach of **Platja des Grau**, avoiding the roped-off dunes, then cross a footbridge to return to **Es Grau**.

WALK 16

s'Albufera des Grau

Start/Finish	Centre de Interpretació
Distance	6km (3¾ miles)
Total Ascent/Descent	150m (490ft)
Time	2hrs
Terrain	Easy tracks over low hills near a lagoon.
Refreshments	None.
Public transport	None.

The lagoon of s'Albufera des Grau is the centrepiece of the Parc Natural de s'Albufera des Grau, which stretches from Es Grau to Addaia. The reserve also includes an attractive coastline, low hills, patchy woodlands and a few farms. There is an interpretation centre just to the south of the lagoon, and two short and easy waymarked trails: itinerari 1 and itinerari 2. Both of these can be followed along the southern shore, passing bird hides. There is another short trail, itinerari 3, that can be followed near the start of Walk 15.

When following the Me-5 road towards the little village of Es Grau, turn left as signposted for the **Parc Natural s'Albufera des Grau**, reaching a car park at the **Centre de Interpretació**. ▶ Where the road forks keep left as signposted 'accés itineraries 100m', passing through a gap between bush-covered hills to reach another parking space. There are gates to right and left.

Go through the gate on the right to follow itinerari 1, and walk up a stony path where the sandstone bedrock shows through. Almost immediately there is a detour left, leading to Aguait d'en Biel, where there is a bird-watching hide. Pass another gate, walk over a crest and downhill. Rise again for a good view left of the lagoon of s'Albufera des Grau,

Open daily from 0900, closing at either 1500 or 1700. A free detailed leaflet map is available and there are exhibits to see.

97

A bird hide is available just off-route at Aguait d'en Biel

then keep left down past another gate. Cross a dip and rise, with the lagoon now seen to the right, at **Cala de Llimpia**. Return the same way to the parking space.

Go through the other gate to follow itinerari 2 along a track. A screen on the right allows birds to be observed at Pantalla de ses Fonts. Walk gently uphill to a junction and go down to the right. The track crosses a bushy dip, rises over sandstone bedrock and levels out at a junction with a view of the lagoon of s'Albufera des Grau. To the right a detour leads to screens and a bird-watching hide at Aguait de sa Punta de ses Ànedes; go there first, then continue along the other track.

The surroundings are bushy at first, then the track broadens and there are good views of the lagoon. The way narrows, running through bushes again, climbing over a hill to join another track. Turn right downhill, then rise and turn right at a junction. There are more views of the lagoon, as well as screens to the right at Pantalles des Prat, allowing birds to be observed in a marshy area. Walk downhill and turn left at a barrier, cross a slight rise, walk down to a track and keep right to follow it back to the parking space. Walk back to the main car park at the **Centre de Interpretació**.

COAST TO COAST
Maó to Ciutadella

Monte Toro, the highest point on Menorca, is crowned by the Santuari El Toro

INTRODUCTION

Following a track through fields near Sant Antoni de Ruma in central Menorca

It is possible to walk from coast to coast across Menorca, from Maó to Ciutadella, in four fairly easy days, covering a total of 71km (44½ miles). Each stage is of course linear, but the start and finish points for each are served by the most regular bus services on the island.

The first stage is mostly way-marked as the PR-IB-Me 1 trail, and the remainder is often waymarked as a cycleway, including several stretches along minor roads. The route includes an ascent of Monte Toro, the highest point on Menorca, as well as a few rocky gorges and other features of interest, not to mention an abundance of archaeological remains.

Each of the four stages offers a fine day's walk for those who may not wish to follow the entire route.

STAGE 1
Maó to Alcaidús and Alaior

Start	Plaça d'Espanya, Maó
Finish	Bus station, Alaior
Distance	19km (12 miles)
Total Ascent	200m (655ft)
Total Descent	170m (555ft)
Time	6hrs
Terrain	Mostly gentle roads, tracks and paths, but one path in the early stages is quite rugged.
Refreshment	Plenty of choice in Maó and Alaior.
Public transport	Regular daily buses link Maó and Ciutadella with Alaior.

The waymarked PR-IB-Me 1 trail runs from the outskirts of Maó almost to Alcaidús. As this is in the middle of nowhere, with no access to bus services, it is worth continuing along well-walked roads and tracks to the town of Alaior. The route passes, or runs close to, a series of interesting historic and archaeological sites, so allow plenty of time to explore them. They include Sant Joan des Vergers, Fornàs de Torelló, Torellonet Vell, Talatí de Dalt, Navetes de Rafal Rubi and Torralba d'en Salort. Alaior is also worth exploring.

There are many ways to leave the Plaça d'Espanya in **Maó**, and a street map (such as the one at the front of this guide) will prove useful. Walk up to the adjoining Plaça de la Conquesta, where the Biblioteca Pública de l'Estat is located. ▶ Turn left along the narrow cobbled Carrer d'Alfons III and continue straight along Carrer de Sant Roc, passing through a big 14th century stone gateway called the Portal de Sant Roc.

Walk straight along S'Arraval and the road rises, reaching a crossroads. Turn right onto Carrer del Sol, then turn quickly left up Carrer de Santa Victòria. Go across a roundabout and walk straight along Camí de Dalt de Sant Joan. Cross a road on the edge of the city to reach a mapboard, which marks the start of the **PR-IB-Me 1** trail.

There are two nearby viewpoints overlooking Port de Maó.

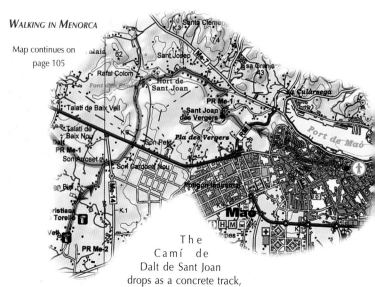

Map continues on page 105

The track overlooks a flat and fertile valley.

The Camí de Dalt de Sant Joan drops as a concrete track, rises as a cobbled track and becomes grassy as it meanders past fields. Drop to a busy main road and carefully cross to the other side, to continue along a track as marked. ◄ Descend on concrete and bare limestone to a cobbled square, where the whitewashed *ermita* of **Sant Joan des Vergers** is located. Steep wooded slopes and cliffs rise nearby.

Walk along a road as marked, gently up and down, passing fields and farms. Cross a bridge over the Torrent des Gorg and turn left to follow a road upstream, the Camí de sa Font d'en Simó, passing lots of bridges. Cross the river at the end of the road, at Verger d'es Gorg, and follow a track beside a steep slope of tall holm oaks at Alzinar d'Alfavara. The track narrows to a path, reaching a junction of tracks at **Font d'en Simó**.

Turn left up a grassy track, which suddenly gives way to a rough and rocky path in a well-wooded gorge. The path is basically in a streambed, but some short stretches are cobbled and a longer cobbled stretch later climbs from the gorge to pass fields above. A track leads to the busy Me-1 road at **Son Petit**. Cross over and walk along a quiet narrow road. Go under a bridge carrying the Me-14

The ermita of Sant Joan des Vergers lies on the outskirts of Maó

road to reach a signposted junction, and turn right. ▶ See Walk 7.

A track, the Camí Vell d'Alaior, runs past a surprisingly clean waste treatment plant; it rises, falls and meanders, eventually reaching a road junction, mapboard and signposts. Turn left along the Camí de Talatí, reaching a parking space and a gate for the prehistoric village of **Talatí de Dalt**.

Turning left leads off-route to archaeological sites at Fornàs de Torelló and Torellonet Vell, and the road also links with the PR-IB-Me 2 trail.

TALATÍ DE DALT

Follow a numbered trail around 12 features of interest.

1   Entrance and seasonally-staffed information hut
2   19th-century cistern and cattle watering trough
3   Cave, probably used as a pre-talaiotic burial site
4   Cave, probably used as a pre-talaiotic burial site
5   Small tumbled *talaiot*, with a stone pillar nearby
6   Sanctuary with *taula*, pillars and encircling wall
7   Large central talaiot, collapsed on one side
8   Huddle of talaiotic houses with covered chambers
9   Possibly a small talaiot
10   Remains of a defensive wall around the village
11   A talaiotic house
12   Hypostile chamber, of uncertain purpose

Turning left links with Sant Climent and Walk 7.

Continue walking along the road, rising and falling gently past fields and a few houses, eventually reaching a crossroads, mapboard and signposts at **Algendar**. Turn right to walk down the Camí d'Algendar. ◄ The road passes fields and reaches a mapboard at the end of the PR-IB-Me 1 near the big house of Binifaell Nou. This is in the middle of nowhere, so it is worth extending the walk. Follow the road onwards, reaching a junction near the busy Me-1 road. Either turn left towards Alcaidús and Alaior, but first consider a short detour off-route.

Detour to Rafal Rubí
Cross the busy Me-1 road and go straight down the quiet Camí de Rafal Rubí. A gate on the left is marked for the Navetes de Rafal Rubí. A short field path links two upturned-boat-shaped *navetes*, or family burial chambers, dating from 1500-1000BC. Retrace your steps back across the busy road to the road junction and turn right for Alaior, walking towards houses.

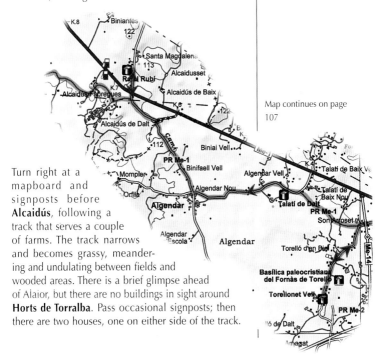

Map continues on page 107

Turn right at a mapboard and signposts before **Alcaidús**, following a track that serves a couple of farms. The track narrows and becomes grassy, meandering and undulating between fields and wooded areas. There is a brief glimpse ahead of Alaior, but there are no buildings in sight around **Horts de Torralba**. Pass occasional signposts; then there are two houses, one on either side of the track.

TORRALBA D'EN SALORT

Follow a numbered trail around 10 features of interest.

1   Hilltop talaiot, damaged and partially collapsed
2   Sanctuary with taula, pillars and encircling wall
3   Small talaiot and pre-talaiotic house foundation
4   Underground silos for storage of food or water
5   Ruins of a 17th century house and small chapel
6   Sandstone quarry with distinctive stepped cuts
7   Talaiotic hypogeums, or tombs, cut into the rock
8   Relatively recent circular threshing floor, or *era*
9   Small section of 'cyclopean' defensive wall
10 Hypostile chamber, possibly used for storage

Join a road and turn right for immediate access to the prehistoric village of **Torralba d'en Salort**.

Follow the road onwards, first downhill, then rising and falling, with occasional views of Alaior ahead. An old building lies to the left on a rise at **Santa Ana des**

Rafal. Eventually the road passes beneath a bridge carrying the busy Me-1 road, and enters the little town of **Alaior**. Keep walking straight ahead, until a turning has to be made at the end of Carrer de Cala en Busquets. Either turn right to reach the bus stops, or turn left to explore further around town (banks with ATMs, post office, shops, bars, restaurants, buses, taxis).

To head straight for the bus stops, first turn right, then turn left into a car park. Look for a blue circular pedestrian sign that indicates a path flanked by grass, shortcutting the road, heading straight for bus stops and taxis on Carrer Joan Baptista de la Salle.

To explore around town instead, first turn left, then turn right up Carrer de sa Bassa Roja. At the top continue along the pedestrianised Carrer des Coll des Palmer, to reach the Plaça de la Constitució. Head left along the narrow Carrer Menor to reach the hilltop church of Sant Eulàlia. Double back to Plaça de la Constitució and turn left down Carrer des Forn and Carrer des Banyer, passing the Convent de Sant Diego. Turn left onto Carrer Joan Baptista de la Salle to finish at the bus stops and taxis.

STAGE 2
Alaior to Monte Toro and Es Mercadal

Start	Carrer Joan Baptista de la Salle, Alaior
Finish	Carrer des Migjorn, Es Mercadal
Distance	16km (10 miles)
Total Ascent	400m (1310ft)
Total Descent	400m (1310ft)
Time	5hrs
Terrain	Mostly easy, along quiet roads and tracks through cultivated countryside. One track may be flooded and one path is steep and rugged.
Refreshment	Plenty of choice in Alaior and Es Mercadal. Bar restaurant on top of Monte Toro.
Public transport	Regular daily buses serve Alaior and Es Mercadal from Maó and Ciutadella. Fewer buses serve Es Mercadal from Arenal d'en Castell.

The summit of Monte Toro stands only 362m (1188ft) above sea level, but it is the highest point on Menorca. It is crowned by fortifications, a church and a restaurant. Cars and tour buses can be driven up the mountain, but there are very few paths nearby that walkers can use. However, this route approaches the mountain from Alaior, using quiet roads and farm tracks; after climbing to the summit it simply follows a winding road down to Es Mercadal.

Start at the bus stops on Carrer Joan Baptista de la Salle in **Alaior** (banks with ATMs, post office, shops, bars, restaurants, buses, taxis). Walk towards the town and turn right up Carrer des Banyer, passing the Convent de San Diego. Continue straight up the pedestrianised Carrer des Forn, enter the Plaça de la Constitució and turn right along Carrer Menor. Walk up to the church of Sant Eulàlia and keep walking up Carrer des Retxats. The moment the road levels out, turn left along Carrer des Grillons. Turn right down a narrow passage into Plaça Nova, where palm trees grow, and walk diagonally across it. Go down stone steps and walk straight along Es Camí Nou.

The road rises to a pine-shaded playground and the 18th century chapel of Sant Pere Nou. ▶ Turn left behind the chapel to follow a road signposted as a cycleway to Es Mercadal, along the Camí de Biniuarda Vell. Quickly turn right and continue straight ahead, following road flanked by walls past fields, down to a junction. Turn left along a narrower road signposted as the Camí des Migjorn. This runs down, up, then down again to pass Estancia den Agusti.

The road runs uphill again and turns left on top of the hill, so keep straight ahead as signposted down a track instead. The fields on either side give way to woods, which include pines and holm oaks. The track rises, then makes a longer descent, emerging from the woods into more fields, crossing a bridge over a stream. ▶ Continue along the track, parallel to the stream, reaching a sign-posted junction. Turn right and the track is sometimes worn to bare rock on the **Plans d'Alaior**, and as it runs lower than the fields alongside, it can get wet and muddy after rain.

A road is reached – the military road known as the **Camí d'en Kane**. ▶ Turn left to follow it, passing a cycleway mapboard at a turning for the Casa de Colònies Santa Eularieta. Continue straight along the road, passing entrances to the farms of s'Astansia,

There is a post office across the road, and the tower of a former windmill on the edge of town.

Note Monte Toro rising to the right.

Kane was an 18th-century British Governor of Menorca.

Map continues on page 111

109

A track is worn down to bare rock on the way to the military road of Camí d'en Kane

Bini Llobet and **s'Aranjassa**, the latter having the appearance of a little hilltop village. Walk down the road, noting a track down to the right for Sant Joan de la Creu. Don't take this, but take the very next turning on the right, for Son Carlos.

Go up the farm road, and when it turns right, keep straight ahead up a grassy, stony track signposted 'accés peatonal al Toro'. This rises, levels out, then rises again to a small gate. Go straight through and climb rougher, rockier and steeper terrain, eventually reaching a clear track. Turn right to follow it past a gate and reach a road. Turn right to follow this bendy road to the top of **Monte Toro**, passing 'km2' and 'km3' markers. ◄

There are views of surrounding farms, fields and forests, as well as the settlements of Es Mercadal and Fornells.

At the summit of **Monte Toro** go through an arch into the Santuari El Toro, to reach the Bar Restaurante Sa Posada del Toro, a fine courtyard, church, gift shop and old square stone tower. Look inside the restaurant to see an old monastic refectory. The best views from the summit are from the Mirador de Ponent, where buses park, and the Mirador de Tramuntana, where cars park. The view from the restaurant terrace is mediocre, while the worst view is from a statue of Christ, on a taula-like plinth, looking towards an ugly array of communications masts.

Walk back down the road, the Carrer Virgen de Monte Toro, charting progress by watching for the 'km3' marker, where there is rock and scrub, followed by pines. Pass the 'km2' marker, where there is a view of quarries, and go down around a bend in a rock cutting, taking note of a little mural concerning the height of the mountain. Pass the 'km1' marker, where a farmhouse to the right is called Peu del Toro. The road leads down to a roundabout on the edge of **Es Mercadal** (accommodation, banks with ATMs, post office, shops, bars restaurants, buses, taxis).

Looking down on a huddle of farm buildings from the road onto Monte Toro

111

Molí d'es Racó atop a restaurant in Es Mercadel.

To reach the bus stop, walk straight down from the roundabout, through the Plaça de Pare Camps, then turn left along Avinguda del Mestre Garí. The bus stop is at a junction with the Carrer des Migjorn. If there is time to explore the town centre in the other direction from Plaça de Pare Camps, then visit the Molí d'en Biel, Ferreria d'en Carretero, church of Sant Martí and a restaurant crowned by the fine windmill of Molí d'es Racó.

STAGE 3

Es Mercadal to Ferreries

Start	Carrer des Migjorn, Es Mercadal
Finish	Snack Bar Vimpi, Ferreries
Distance	17km (10½ miles); extension: 3km (2 miles)
Total Ascent	260m (855ft)
Total Descent	230m (755ft)
Time	5hrs; extension: 1 hour there and back
Terrain	Easy walking, mostly quiet roads through gentle countryside and low hills, with one stretch of track.
Refreshment	Plenty of choice in Es Mercadal and Ferreries.
Public transport	Regular daily buses link Es Mercadal and Ferreries with Maó and Ciutadella. Fewer buses serve Es Mercadal from Arenal d'en Castell.

This route, between the little towns of Es Mercadal and Ferreries, is mostly along quiet roads signposted as a cycleway, with one stretch along a track. Gentle countryside is traversed, passing dairy farms, and some roads running northwards are signposted for remote beaches, which are visited on the GR223 Stage 8. Later, the route crosses low hills, where there are woods and bushy scrub. The descent to Ferreries passes Hort de Sant Patrici, where cheese and wine are produced.

Start at the bus stop in **Es Mercadal**, where Carrer des Migjorn joins the Avinguda del Mestre Garí. Walk straight along the Avinguda del Mestre Garí, passing the Plaça del Pare Camps, continuing along the brick-paved Carrer Nou. Pass the tiny Plaça de la Constitució and walk along Carrer de Baix. Cross a river using a bridge called Pont de Baix, then turn right to follow Carrer Tramuntana. ▶ Follow the road to a roundabout on the edge of town and turn right as signposted for 'Platges Costa Nord'.

A lovely country road has a curious building to the left at Sa Fontassa: a late 19th century wash-house. Also note a farm to the right with a windmill tower, the Molí

Note an old smithy, Ferreria d'en Carretero, just before the bridge, and Molí d'en Biel just after it.

113

WALKING IN MENORCA

de Tramuntana. There are low rolling hills and several dairy farms. The road undulates gently and is flanked by sandstone walls. Pass a signpost and note water treatment lagoons to the right, then pass another signpost at **Barbatxi**. Eventually reach a road junction at Ses Tres Boques, where there is a mapboard illustrating the 'Camins de Tramuntana', showing which roads and tracks can be followed to a series of north coast beaches.

It is possible to see the distant lighthouse on Cap de Cavalleria to the north.

Keep left, in effect straight ahead, as signposted for cyclists. The road crosses a rise at **Montpalau**. ◀ Cross another rise near the farm of **Binialcalà**, then follow the road down through big fields where the farms seem distant. There is a view of the little mountain of Santa Àgueda, and there is sometimes a view back along the undulating road to Monte Toro. Pass the access

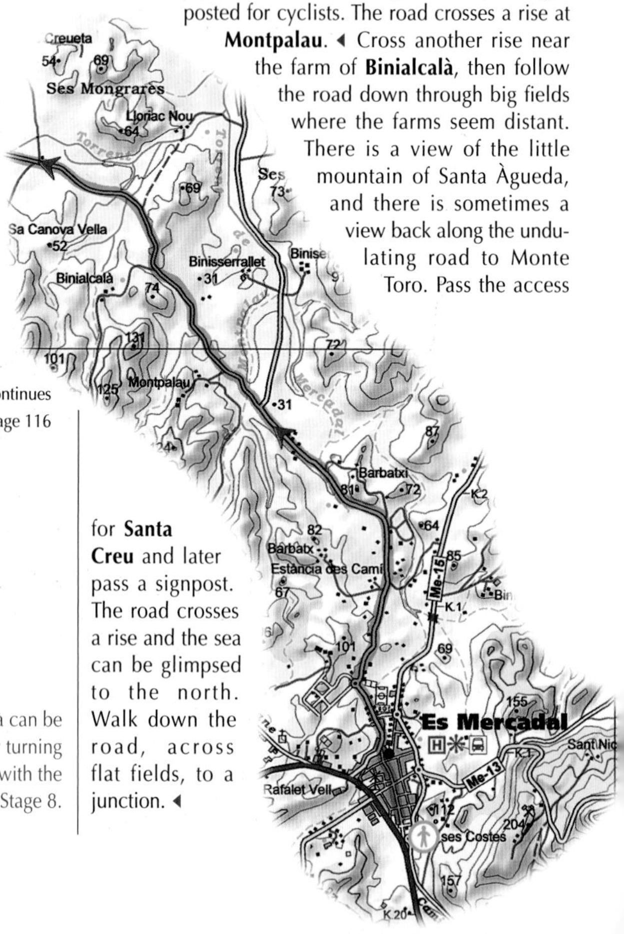

Map continues on page 116

for **Santa Creu** and later pass a signpost. The road crosses a rise and the sea can be glimpsed to the north. Walk down the road, across flat fields, to a junction. ◀

Binimel.là can be reached by turning right, linking with the GR223 Stage 8.

114

Fields and low hills seen from the road near Ses Tres Boques

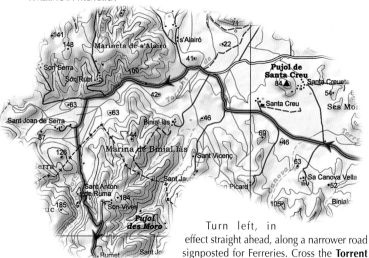

Map continues
on page 118

Turn left, in effect straight ahead, along a narrower road signposted for Ferreries. Cross the **Torrent de s'Alairó** and follow the road over another little rise. Ignore a turnoff to the right marked as private, and continue on the road as it winds and climbs into a valley. Fields are now small and the slopes are densely wooded, with wild olives and a few pines, dense lentisc bushes, gorse and càrritx. Reach the end of the tarmac, where a gate on the right bars access to **Son Rubí**.

Keep left, or straight ahead, down a track past a cycleway mapboard with Santa Àgueda rising ahead. Walk down a bit and up a bit to a junction and a signpost, and turn left downhill to cross a stream. The track climbs between fields, and the white hilltop farm of **Sant Joan de Serra** is in view. Pass a signpost, walk ahead and go round a left bend. Walk along and up a track to go through a gate onto the property of **Sant Antoni de Ruma**. This stretch is not flanked by walls, but stay on the track, crossing a stream in a slight dip.

There is a view of the sea to the north again, and Monte Toro can also be seen.

The bendy track climbs to a farm and a tarmac road-end. Turn left up the road, climbing steeply on slopes of pine and càrritx. Go through a gate at the top, where there is a cycleway mapboard and a gateway to **Son Vives**. ◀ The road continues rising past fields and bushy scrub. There is a building to the right, and the farm of Ruma Vell to the left. Pass a signpost and keep left for Ferreries, possibly glimpsing Mallorca in the distance, before reaching the highest part of the road, around 220m (720ft).

Follow the road downhill, crossing a dip on the way past **Sant Rafal**, then go up past a signpost and keep left, crossing a crest on the way past **Son Pere**. ▶ Walk down a steep, bendy concrete road. The lower slopes are mostly covered in wild olives and càrritx, while the higher slopes are wooded. The road becomes tarmac as it drops past small farms and cultivated plots in the bottom of a valley. Pass a junction with the Camí de la Marcona, and again keep left for Ferreries. Pass the lovely grounds of Hort de Sant Patrici, where cheese and wine are produced.

There is a brief glimpse of Ferreries ahead.

Three types of cheese are produced at **Hort de Sant Patrici**, according to how long they are matured. 'Tierno' requires a minimum of 21 days to produce. 'Semicurado' is matured for two to three months. 'Curado' matures for as long as eight or nine months. The site includes the mansion-like Ca Na Xini hotel, a restaurant, a cheese museum and a shop

Hort de Sant Patrici, where cheese is made, can be visited before reaching Ferreries

specialising in cheese, wine and olive oil (tel 971-373702, **www.santpatrici.com**).

The winding road passes a farm and a signpost, then runs beneath the main Me-1 road. Keep straight ahead; there is an industrial area to the left and smallholdings to the right. Reach a roundabout on the outskirts of **Ferreries** (accommodation, banks with ATMs, post office, shops, bars, restaurants, buses, taxis) and turn right. Walk only to the next roundabout, where the bus stop is beside the Snack Bar Vimpi.

Ferreries is named after the blacksmiths who settled here, in the centre of Menorca, where they could be sure to catch the passing trade – especially pack-horses. The Centre de la Naturaleza de Menorca, on Carrer Mallorca, is open on Saturdays.

Extension to Ermita de Ferreries

Leave the bus stop and Snack Bar Vimpi, walk round the corner and down a road past the post office (*Correos*). Reach a crossroads with the Avinguda Son Morera and go straight across a bridge over a river. (A nearby old stone-arch bridge can be crossed instead, which is the 'traditional' route.) Walk along a brick-paved road and climb concrete steps into a wood of holm oaks and pines.

Turn right up a path, noting the painted religious 'stations' on boulders. Turn left up another path, which soon turns right and broadens, and one stretch is concrete. Climb a stony, bouldery path, with a couple of short downhill stretches, mostly flanked by dense, bushy scrub, heather and cistus. Other parts of the path are patched with concrete before reaching the **Ermita de Ferreries**, which has its own square and well. ◄ Retrace your steps back down to town.

There are views down to Ferreries, with Sant Patrici close to hand, while Monte Toro and Es Migjorn Gran are more distant.

118

STAGE 4
Ferreries to Ciutadella

Start	Snack Bar Vimpi, Ferreries
Finish	Plaça dels Pins, Ciutadella
Distance	19km (12 miles)
Total Ascent	200m (655ft)
Total Descent	270m (885ft)
Time	6hrs
Terrain	Farm tracks across low hills and valleys, with one short rocky path. Easy road-walking afterwards, apart from paths used for off-route detours.
Refreshment	Plenty of choice in Ferreries and Ciutadella, but nothing in-between, apart from three farms selling cheese.
Public transport	Regular daily buses link Ferreries and Ciutadella with Maó.

The gorge of Barranc d'Algendar can be reached by following farm tracks from Ferreries, then descending through a deep narrow cleft called the Pas d'en Revull. For many walkers, this is a fine destination in its own right, and then they return to Ferreries. However, it is worth continuing to Ciutadella, mostly along roads, making short detours to archaeological sites at Torre Trencada, Naveta des Tudons and Talaiot de Montefí. Interesting quarries are sometimes open at Pedreres de s'Hostal near Ciutadella.

Start from the bus stop at the Snack Bar Vimpi in **Ferreries**, and walk along the Avinguda Verge del Toro, which leads to the Plaça Espanya. ▸ Walk straight up the short Costa d'es Convent, quickly turn right along Carrer Degá Febrer, then left up Plaça Jaume II. This leads into the Pla de l'Església, to the entrance of Sant Bartomeu church. Leave the top of the plaça up a brick-paved street, climbing steps to a busy road junction at a large house called Ses Delícies.

A detour left leads to the Centre de la Naturaleza de Menorca, which is on nearby Carrer Mallorca.

Follow the road signposted for Ciutadella and Sta Galdana, using the raised and railed footway beside the road. Turn left up Carrer del Camp and walk straight

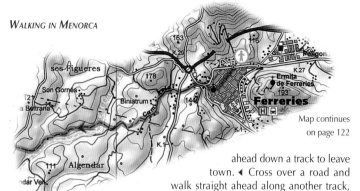

Map continues
on page 122

ahead down a track to leave town. ◄ Cross over a road and walk straight ahead along another track, signposted as **Camí Reial** and 'accés al Barranc d'Algendar'. Most of the climbing is on concrete, flanked by holm oaks; a crest is crossed after **Biniatrum**, passing fields and a farm.

Note the wells on the left, called Es Pouets.

Turn right as signposted for Ciutadella, down a walled path shaded by holm oaks, on bare limestone at first, then trodden earth. Cross a dip and pass a sign-post, climbing a little to pass a cross called Sa Creu de Son Gornes, erected in 1865. Walk downhill, often on limestone bedrock, then the smooth and level path is raised as it runs between fields in the shallow **Barranc d'Algendaret**. The path climbs, then undulates alongside the valley, often shaded by trees, while the limestone bedrock is sometimes grooved.

A derelict house on the left is completely overgrown.

◄ The path rises through a little gap cut from the limestone, where the cave of Sa Cova Reial has been cut. The path rises past a notice for Sa Costa de na Salema, where there are tree roots and lumpy limestone. Reach a junction where a tarmac road heads right and a concrete road runs straight ahead downhill. Follow the concrete road as signposted for Ciutadella, until a gateway on the left at the bottom gives way to a track running through fields. Alternatively, stay on the concrete road to avoid the Pas d'en Revull.

Turn left along a path where there is a cliff to the left and a wall to the right. The limestone cliff often overhangs, but the path is easy. Turn right down a steepening rocky path where it can be slippery underfoot. Pass cliffs and huge boulders, where overhangs are often so pronounced that the

The narrow Pas d'en Revull leads down to the Barranc d'Algendar

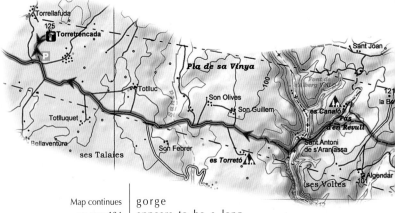

Map continues
on page 124

Note cave houses in
a rock wall.

Make a short
detour left here,
to see a mossy
charcoal hearth
and an overhanging
limestone cliff.

gorge
appears to be a long
cave. This is the **Pas d'en Revull**, and a few stone steps
have been added to ease the way through. Go through a
gate at the bottom to join a track in a valley, then turn left
down the track. ◄ Limestone cliffs rise on both sides, and
when the farm of **Sant Antoni de s'Aranjassa** is reached,
one of these cliffs terminates as a tower of rock.

The track continues down through the **Barranc
d'Algendar** and becomes a boulder-paved path, uneven
underfoot, with a stream alongside on the right. Cross
the stream using a slab footbridge to reach a signpost
on the other side. Climb the boulder-paved path, passing through a rock cutting, and noticing a large holm oak
tree on the left. ◄ Keep climbing up the densely-wooded
slope, following the path hammered through little cliffs,
eventually passing a ruin with twin-arched doorways.
A signpost points ahead for Ciutadella. Follow a walled
track, reaching a broad crest and a road at a gateway to
Son Guiem.

Follow the road gently down and note a left turn
for es Torretó. However, walk ahead gently up the road,
crossing a crest where there is a little stone cross to the
right near Torreta Saura. Cross a big dip in the road and
note a well and a trough to the left. Walk uphill and keep
straight ahead at a junction. The road descends and rises
gently, passing a signpost at Tot Lluch. As usual, keep
walking ahead for Ciutadella. Later, pass a broad level
area where there is a locked gate to the left and, soon

afterwards, pass a junction where the road bends left and is signposted for Ciutadella. On the right there is a car park for the archaeological site of **Torre Trencada**.

TORRE TRENCADA

Leave the car park through a little gate incorporating a small cattle grid, then follow a field path through a couple more gates. The archaeological site is quite rugged and largely overgrown by wild olives, but it can be explored using a numbered trail.

1	Burial cave
2	Taula with two supporting columns
3	Talaiot
4	Burial cave
5	Hypostyle (storage room)
6	Aljub (Cistern)
7	Graves and water collection ponds
8	Re-used stone tables and benches from the site

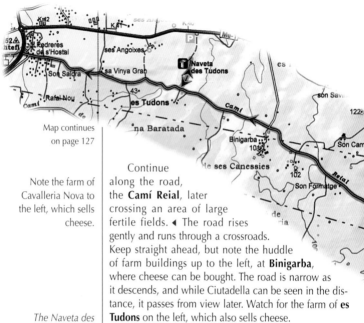

Map continues
on page 127

Note the farm of
Cavalleria Nova to
the left, which sells
cheese.

Continue
along the road,
the **Camí Reial**, later
crossing an area of large
fertile fields. ◀ The road rises
gently and runs through a crossroads.
Keep straight ahead, but note the huddle
of farm buildings up to the left, at **Binigarba**,
where cheese can be bought. The road is narrow as
it descends, and while Ciutadella can be seen in the distance, it passes from view later. Watch for the farm of **es
Tudons** on the left, which also sells cheese.

*The Naveta des
Tudons is an
iconic Menorcan
archaeological site*

To visit the **Naveta des Tudons** from here go through
a gate and cross a cattle grid, following a track

worn to bedrock past bushes and grassy patches. The Naveta des Tudons lies to the left, in a modern walled enclosure, and has the appearance of an upturned boat hull. It was probably built around 1500BC, and contains a lower and upper chamber inside its thick stone walls. When excavated it was discovered to contain around 100 skeletons and assorted artefacts.

Follow the road onwards, passing Ses Tanques Ramon I Bosch, on the right, and then a signpost on the left pointing ahead for Ciutadella. Later, pass Rafal des Morer, a composting site, and heaps of rock and rubble. The quarries of Pedrera de Marès lie on both sides of the road at Son Salord, then a mini roundabout is reached where the quarries of 'Lithica' lie to the right, at **Pedreres de s'Hostal**.

Pedreres de s'Hostal is a soft sandstone quarry, with strikingly geometrical square-cut walls, which was closed in 1994. It has been preserved and enhanced as an attraction, featuring quarrying techniques and machinery, as well as an amazing garden on the quarry floor. The Lithica project, tel 971-481578, www.lithica.es, manages the site and offers occasional tours.

The road swings left, but drop down instead and climb steeply beneath a concrete bridge carrying the busy **Rc-2 road** past Ciutadella. The road ahead was dug up by archaeologists, down to limestone bedrock, and a short gravel path runs alongside. At the end of this, it is worth making a detour to the right to visit the archaeological site of Talaiot de Montefí.

Talaiot de Montefí has yet to be 'developed', but can be explored with due regard to the rugged

Overlooking the head of the narrow harbour in the interesting little city of Ciutadella

ground underfoot, and a noticeboard indicates the main features. There are three small talaiots and the ruins of a fourth, as well as burial sites and small caves. It appears that the site was occupied from the early Bronze Age to the time of the Roman conquest.

Follow the road onwards, gently down past the outskirts of **Ciutadella**.

There is a cemetery to the left, then pass straight through a crossroads, and later note a sports complex to the right. A cycleway accompanies the road towards the city. Cross a busy road and continue straight along a quiet

road. Turn right at the end, then quickly left to continue along Camí de Maó. This reaches the Plaça Alfons III; either continue straight into the centre to explore or, if intending to catch a bus, turn left along Avinguda Jaume I. This leads onto Avinguda Capita Negret, which in turn reaches Plaça dels Pins. There are some bus stops on the far side, but turn left for Plaça Menorca for buses to Maó and Es Migjorn Gran.

GR223
Camí de Cavalls

The GR223 heads inland from Cap de Menorca, climbing to a rugged viewpoint (Stage 6)

INTRODUCTION

Low cliff coast and rocky headlands on the way to Cova dels Pardals (Stage 4)

The long-distance GR223, or Camí de Cavalls, is fully waymarked and makes a complete circuit around Menorca. As such, it can be started or finished at any point, but the likelihood is that most walkers will choose to start and finish in the island capital of Maó. The Menorcan government promotes the route as an anti-clockwise circuit, broken into 20 stages. This guidebook, however, describes the route in a clockwise direction, in 10 stages that each equate to a reasonable day's walk. The easier southern coast is walked first; careful planning is required along the more remote northern coast.

While much of the route runs along the coast, significant stretches run further inland and have no view of

the sea. The route is loosely based on a centuries-old path encircling the island, which was used to allow horse-riders to be quickly despatched to respond to any threat of invasion. No-one knows when the route was created, but it has been referred to throughout the centuries. When many stretches were enclosed by landowners, local walkers and horse-riders mounted a very strong campaign to re-open the route. This occasionally involved mass trespasses and the physical dismantling of walls blocking the route. The Menorcan government passed a law to restore the route as far as practicable, funding all the necessary work, and completed it all in just 10 years.

Any stretch of the Camí de Cavalls can be used as a day-walk, simply by ensuring that there is bus access at either end of each stretch, by arranging drop-offs and pick-ups with friends or by using taxis. Long-distance walkers, however, must decide whether they intend to commute to and from each stage from a fixed base, or walk from place to place and organise accommodation along the way. Both approaches will work, providing that care is taken to study bus timetables and accommodation provision. Most of the places reached at the end of the day are small resorts, where the hotels only operate fully during the peak summer season.

True backpacking, where walkers carry tents, sleeping bags and all the kit they need to be self-sufficient, is difficult because there are no campsites on the route. Wild camping is illegal, and even if it were to be considered, it would have to be undertaken in a very, very discreet manner. If you watch other walkers on the trail, it is clear that some of them are carrying full backpacking kit, and the assumption must be made that they are camping wild.

Once a plan has been formulated, it is simply a case of following the trail, which is very well waymarked and signposted. The standard 'European' marking system of red and white stripes is used, and the words 'Camí de Cavalls' and 'GR223' feature regularly. Olive-wood gates, flanked by stout stone piers, have been designed so that they open easily and

shut securely afterwards. It is never necessary to climb walls or fences. A little more care needs to be taken when passing through built-up areas, where there are lots of distractions and it is easy to miss a turning.

Almost every stage described in this book can be achieved comfortably in a day's walk, but there is a very long gap with no accommodation along the remote and rugged north coast of Menorca. For the sake of breaking the route at some point allowing vehicle access, the remote beach at els Alocs has been chosen, but it is important to arrange a pick-up at that point. Only the strongest walkers, willing to start early and finish late, can hope to walk the full distance from Cala Morell to Cala Tirant in a day.

Opportunities to buy food and drink along the trail are mentioned, but it is wise to carry sufficient provisions for each day's walk just in case the places mentioned are closed. In the event of difficulty at any point, either head for the nearest place with a bus service, in order to leave the route, or remember that a taxi can be called to any public road simply by phoning 971-367111.

The best map of the Camí de Cavalls is produced by Editorial Alpina www.editorialalpina.com, at a scale of 1:50,000, used throughout this guidebook, on which the GR223 route is marked.

STAGE 1
Maó to Binissafúller

Start	Plaça d'Espanya, Maó
Finish	Binissafúller
Distance	20km (12½ miles)
Total Ascent/Descent	210m (690ft)
Time	8hrs
Terrain	Mostly easy, along roads, tracks and clear paths passing urban areas, fields and woods. Only a few short steep ascents and descents.
Refreshment	Plenty of choice in Maó and Es Castell. Seasonal bar restaurants in Alcalfar and Punta Prima. Bar restaurant in Binissafúller.
Public transport	Regular daily buses link Maó and Es Castell. Summer buses serve s'Algar, Alcalfar, Punta Prima, Binibèquer and Binissafúller.

The Camí de Cavalls leaves Maó by a very direct route, using a busy road to reach Es Castell. This was of course the 'historical' route, but it can be avoided by using the longer coastal route described in Walk 1. Beyond Cala de Sant Esteve and Fort de Marlborough, tracks and paths reach an inlet at Alcalfar, then a coastal path leads to Punta Prima. Much of the route to Binissafúller follows urban coastal roads, passing the intriguing village of Binibèquer Vell.

There are many ways to leave the Plaça d'Espanya in **Maó**, and a street map (such as the one at the front of this guide) will prove useful. Walk up through the adjoining Plaça del Carme into Plaça Princep. Follow the Camí des Castell, leading straight to the edge of the city, to a roundabout on the Me-2 road. Go straight down the main road towards the head of an inlet, **Cala Figuera**.

The road rises and passes a GR223 signpost. Keep straight ahead at a roundabout, or use an underpass to visit a shop, restaurant and hostal at **Son Vilar**. There is a broad pavement beside the road, passing a round tower

Although there is a GR223 signpost across the roundabout, there is no pavement on that side.

and another roundabout, before skirting **Es Castell** (hotels, shops, bar restaurants). Either head left to explore the little town, or continue along the main road from a roundabout and bus stop at Plaça de S'Arraval Vella. ◄

The road has a broad pavement alongside and eventually reaches a crossroads. **Sol de l'Est** lies to the left, but walk straight ahead as signposted for Fort de Marlborough, past a cemetery. Reach a signposted junction and turn right, noting Castillo de San Felipe ahead, an occupied 18th-century fort. Walk along and down the road, passing fields, then fork right down a broad path flanked by bushes. This is bendy and cobbled and avoids using the road to reach the narrow inlet of **Cala de Sant Esteve**.

The coast road can be followed further to reach the cave-like entrance to Fort de Marlborough, an early 18th-century British redoubt.

Turn right to follow the road round the head of the inlet, but watch for the GR223 up to the right on Camí de sa Cala de Sant Esteve. ◄ Pass a mapboard and climb on broken cobbles and bare limestone. The path becomes gentler, flanked by walls and bushes as it passes fields.

The Camí de Cavalls can begin with an exploration of the city of Maó

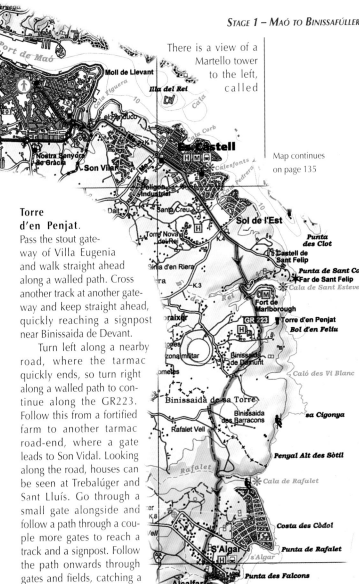

There is a view of a Martello tower to the left, called

Map continues on page 135

Torre d'en Penjat.
Pass the stout gateway of Villa Eugenia and walk straight ahead along a walled path. Cross another track at another gateway and keep straight ahead, quickly reaching a signpost near Binissaida de Devant.

Turn left along a nearby road, where the tarmac quickly ends, so turn right along a walled path to continue along the GR223. Follow this from a fortified farm to another tarmac road-end, where a gate leads to Son Vidal. Looking along the road, houses can be seen at Trebalúger and Sant Lluís. Go through a small gate alongside and follow a path through a couple more gates to reach a track and a signpost. Follow the path onwards through gates and fields, catching a

133

Note a track on the left after a gate that can be used to reach a rocky inlet at Caló de Rafalet.

The resort of s'Algar is to the left.

glimpse of buildings before dropping into the wooded **Barranc de Rafalet**. ◄

Cross the bottom of the valley, where a track is raised on stone supports. Climb past a quarry, often walking on bedrock among pines and holm oak. Cross a crest and descend from the forest, passing buildings, and the Camí de Rafalet reaches a road. ◄ Cross over and walk straight ahead, down a bit, then up a track to a road and a signpost. Turn left along the road and note the Ermita de Sant Esteve down to the right. Turn right as signposted 'Xuroy', down into the little village of **Alcalfar** (bars and summer buses nearby).

Cross the little sandy beach at the head of **Cala Alcalfar**, go through a little gateway, then climb limestone rock-steps on a wooded slope. Turn left and continue as marked, with views across the inlet to the village. The path is flanked by scrub woodland and lentisc bushes, rising and falling to reach another rocky inlet. A signpost points through a gap in a stone wall, and there is a well nearby. ◄ Climb through the scrub containing euphorbia and cistus, as well as juniper.

There is an optional detour to the Martello tower of Torre d'Alcalfar.

The path runs close to a limestone platform that has been pounded by the sea, leaving it covered in big slabs of rock that have been flipped onto it during mighty storms. Go through a gate and walk straight along a coastal road at **Punta Prima** (summer accommodation, shops, bar restaurants, buses, taxis).

Head inland by road, up Costa de sa Torre, as posted for the

134

Torre de Son Ganxo. Instead of going to the tower, pick up and follow a path beside the rugged shore, overlooked by a row of houses called Ses Casetes de Vora Mar. Turn right inland at a signpost, up the short Carrer de sea Tempestes, then turn left along the road, Passeig de sa Torre. Follow this through **Son Ganxo** and continue along Carrer de sa Marina, where there is a restaurant, and Passeig de sa Marina. The road turns

The large sandy beach of Platja de Punta Prima on the south-east corner of Menorca

round the inlet of **Cala Biniancolla** (restaurants, bus stop). ▶

One stretch of the coastal road is free of development, later becoming Carrer de S'Oronella and

Walk 4 joins here. ▶

Map continues on page 137

A peculiar huddle of whitewashed buildings at Binibequer Vell

passing a restaurant on the way to **Biniancolla**. Walk along a broad pavement, passing a little rocky inlet and a small white hut or house. Turn left at a signposted road junction to follow the Camí de s'Anfós Blau through the built-up **Binibèquer Nou**. The road turns round the inlet of **Cala Binibèquer**, rising to Cala Torret, where there are shops and bar restaurants. A broad path can be followed down to a pine-shaded picnic area and sandy beach, and another path can be used to return to the road. Continue along the main road and go straight ahead at a roundabout. Follow the Passeig Marítim past a shop and bar restaurants to reach **Binibèquer Vell** (bar restaurants, shops, hotel, ATM, taxis).

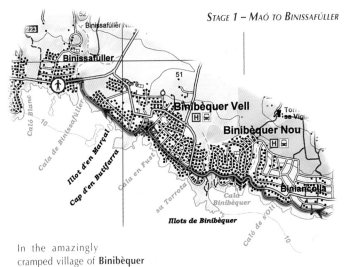

In the amazingly
cramped village of **Binibèquer
Vell** everything is blindingly white, from floor
to chimney tops. Thankfully, traffic is barred and
the centre is pedestrianised. Feel free to explore,
squeezing through narrow alleys and passages,
between and beneath buildings, returning to the
centre afterwards.

Leave the village by heading inland, up a road past a
taxi rank. Turn sharp left down a road to reach a narrow
inlet. Turn right and climb steps marked as 'paso pub-
lico', walking on wooden decking later, before climbing
to a road at a Camí de Cavalls notice. Turn left to follow the road along the coast, away from an Aparthotel.
The Passeig de la Mar runs beside a rocky, scrubby coast
where there are rocky islets, until the road ends abruptly.
A coastal path pushes alongside the inlet of **Cala
de Binissafúller**. Reach a road and go down to the head
of the inlet, crossing a sandy beach. Climb steps and
turn right along a broad path, Carrer de sa Platja, up to
a road and signpost. Turn left along the road through
Binissafúller, reaching a bus stop. ▶

The Bar Restaurante
Binisafua is nearby, if
breaking the journey
at this point and if
there is time to spare
before catching a
bus.

STAGE 2
Binissafúller to Son Bou

Start	Binissafúller
Finish	Son Bou
Distance	20km (12½ miles)
Total Ascent/Descent	210m (690ft)
Time	8hrs
Terrain	Mostly easy, along roads, tracks and clear paths passing a few resorts, fields and woods. Only a few short steep ascents and descents.
Refreshment	Bars and restaurants in Binissafúller, es Canutells, Cala en Porter and Son Bou.
Public transport	Regular daily buses serve Cala en Porter. Summer buses serve Binissafúller, es Canutells and Son Bou.

This whole stage of the Camí de Cavalls keeps its distance from the coast, crossing low plateaux and a series of steep-sided valleys. Between the resorts of es Canutells and Cala en Porter, it is worth detouring to Calascoves to see a cave complex that was used for burials. Another detour can be made to see the talaiotic settlement of Torre d'en Galmés. An ancient Christian site lies at the end of this stage, alongside Son Bou.

Starting from the bus stop in **Binissafúller**, follow the road past the Bar Restaurante Binisafua and continue to the edge of the village. A signpost, gate and mapboard stand on the right, where a path climbs over bare limestone, flanked by wild olive trees and lentisc bushes. The path swings left and goes through a gate, well-marked and well-trodden, through a couple of gaps in drystone walls. Go through a gate and turn left along a track, parallel to a sort of race-track circuit. Turn left through another gate and follow a path beside a wall, then cross a road at **Biniparratx**, where there is a signpost.

Follow a path ahead and downhill beside a wall. Turn right later, down beside another wall, then turn left to walk away from it. The path is flanked by dense bushes

Walled tracks, often flanked by trees, are followed around Binidalí

on the way down into a valley. Turn right to walk along the top of a wall-like dam, then turn left through a gap in a wall into woods containing holm oaks. Climb the broad path, at times chiselled into the limestone and go through a gap in a wall. ▶ Meander through low scrub criss-crossed by old walls, reaching a walled track and signpost. Pass a house called Binidalí d'es Camí and turn left at the next house.

Note the pines among scrub woodland.

Follow the most obvious winding track, avoiding others to left and right. Pass a tennis court and turn left where tracks cross, going up to a house, then straight

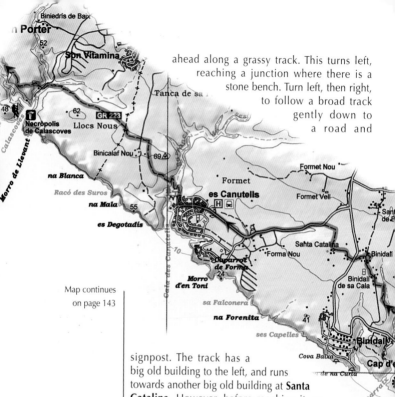

ahead along a grassy track. This turns left, reaching a junction where there is a stone bench. Turn left, then right, to follow a broad track gently down to a road and

Map continues
on page 143

signpost. The track has a big old building to the left, and runs towards another big old building at **Santa Catalina**. However, before reaching it, go through a gate on the right and follow a path through more gates, in and out of fields while heading gently downhill. There are three more big old buildings on the skyline ahead, but the path turns left and heads straight for a gate and road.

Turn left to follow the road past fields and woods; later there are buildings dotted around. On reaching the resort of **es Canutells**, a signpost stands at a road junction. Go straight ahead down a brick-paved road through the Grupotel Mar de Menorca. The Chepas Bar stands to the left, otherwise walk straight down a tarmac road, the Avinguda d'es Canutells. The road ends at the Plaça des Raons, overlooking a cliff-girt inlet. Turn right before this, up Carrer de sa Cala, then turn left into a pine-shaded picnic area. Immediately turn right in front of a building to spot a marker post and a gap in a drystone wall. Follow a path down through woods into the **Barranc de ses Penyes**.

Go through a gate and pass water troughs that are linked together, then follow the path up a wooded slope. Pass a stone shed with feed and water troughs inside. Walk up through a gate and continue up a track, climbing through fields and patchy woods. Reach two gates and go through the one on the right, then follow a wall onwards. Go over a crest, through a gate. ▶ Walk gently down beside a wall and go through a gate, then turn left. There are gates on either side of a track serving the old house, then a signpost.

There is a view of the big old house of Binicalaf Nou to the left.

Follow a meandering path, sometimes following a wall, or going through gaps and gates around **Llocs Nous**. ▶ A gentle descent leads through a gate where there is plenty of càrritx grass alongside. A steeper descent passes cliffs and outcrops on a wooded slope, reaching a track and signpost in a valley bottom near **Calascoves**. To visit the **Necrópolis de Calascoves**, turn left down the track, quickly reaching the attractive rocky inlet. There is a house to the right, and canes grow thickly before a tiny sandy beach is reached.

The houses of Son Vitamina are far to the right, while the houses of Cala en Porter can be seen ahead.

It is worth visiting the **Necrópolis de Calascoves**. The cliffs to the left are dotted with hand-hewn caves that were used for burials. The most sensitive of these are blocked by sheet-iron coverings, but narrow paths and steep flights of rock-steps can be used to visit some of them. Follow yellow arrows

141

A short detour off-route leads to a tiny beach at Calascoves

on a blue background to explore, then retrace your steps back into the valley.

Climb from the valley using a rugged path as signposted for the GR223. Go through a gap in a drystone wall, then follow the wall up through woods. Cross a rise and walk down through a gate. Turn right uphill again and walk through more woods. Drift left from the wall and go down through a gate. A path splits from a track, crosses a dip, then re-joins the track to go through a gap in a wall. Head up to the right as marked, through a gate, and follow the path to go down through another gate. Cross a wooded valley and climb the other side as marked. Go through a gate onto a road with houses alongside.

Turn left along the road, up to a football pitch. Turn right up another road, the Travessera de l'Avinguda Central. This levels out and joins the Avinguda Central where the GR223 turns right. ◄ Follow the road over a rise, across a dip, then over another rise into the centre of **Cala en Porter** (accommodation, supermarkets, ATM, bar restaurants, buses, taxis).

Turning left leads to Cova d'en Xoroi, described at the end of Walk 7.

A complex road junction is reached, where the GR223 goes past the Plaça d'en Mevis, on top of the Centre Civic Cala en Porter, then turns left down the steepest road, the Passeig de la Platja. The road drops through a wooded valley flanked by limestone cliffs, levelling out beside the long curved Hotel Aquarium. ▶

Turn right off the road, past a mapboard, to follow a path beside the reedy **Barranc de Cala en Porter**. The path is sometimes cut into limestone, passing an orchard and becoming a track from a small house to a farmhouse at Huerto Turrobenc Noll. A path zigzags uphill from a signpost, with rustic fencing alongside, cut into the base of a soft and crumbling cliff. Continue through a dip, then the path rises over lumpy limestone, past scrub woodland, with a circular *era*, or tiled threshing floor, to the left.

Walk down a steep slope of scrub woodland to reach the valley bottom, go through a gate and follow

Further along the brick-paved road are bar restaurants, a sandy beach, pools, reed-beds and cliffs.

Map continues on page 144

143

Note the old
farmhouses seen
across the valley on
the way.

the path up to a track and a road. ◄ Turn left down the road and go through a gate and along a track to cross a bridge over a river. Turn left along a narrow tarmac track behind a farmhouse. Turn right as marked along a track, rising through the valley past dense woods and cliffs. Eventually, go up through a gate and reach a track junction on a broad crest at **Comerma de sa Punta**.

A gateway on the left is a private way to Torrenova, so turn right along the track, crossing an open grassy area speckled with daisies. Gates are reached at another junction with a walled track. Turn right to follow this, until a gate and signpost are reached. At this point the GR223 turns left to continue, but it is worth making a detour up the track to **Torre d'en Galmés**.

> **Torre d'en Galmés** is a wonderful prehistoric site. Follow a roped-off concrete path around the highest part, crowned by three *talaiots*. A concrete spur path leads down into an interesting part of the settlement, where there are walls and *taula* enclosures. Follow trodden paths to explore, and note a spur path leading to two caves – one used for burials and one used for storing olive oil. There are plenty of useful explanatory notices.

The GR223 follows a short path down through little fields of asphodel and patchy woods. Cross a footbridge in the **Barranc de Torre Vella** and walk up to a gate and a road.

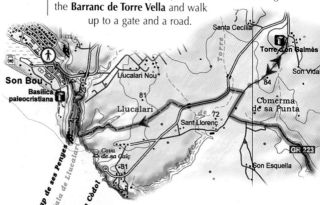

144

Looking down on a ruined palaeo-Christian basilica and the resort of Son Bou

Turn left, and although bushes creep onto the road, views between them reveal little fields. Turn right as signposted through a gate, and a path follows walls through areas of grass, asphodels and patchy woods. The way is well-trodden through gates, meandering uphill, then there is a straight stretch that rises and falls gently, with juniper and pines among the wooded areas around **Llucalari**.

There is a sudden short, steep descent, followed by an ascent and descent among woods. Continue down through a well-wooded rock-walled gorge. Woods give way to bushy scrub and a bouldery bay is reach, flanked by rocky headlands, at **Cala de Llucalari**, where a ruined cave house can be seen. Follow another gorge straight back inland as marked. The path crosses boulders, and scrub gives way to woods with plenty of tall pines. Climb to the left, over a rocky crest. ▶

It is worthwhile turning left off-route for a fine view from a rocky ridge, overlooking a splendid beach, dunes and marshland.

Follow the marked path down through a gate, left a little and down a wooded slope. The path cuts across the slope and doesn't go down to the coast, but a detour can be made in that direction. Although the immediate view is dominated by the large hotel blocks of Sol Milanos Pingüinos, the most interesting feature is a ruined **palaeo-Christian basilica**. The GR223, meanwhile, turns right up a road and left at a junction to pass straight through the resort of **Son Bou** (accommodation, shops, bars, restaurants, ATMs, summer buses, taxis), passing a roundabout. ▶

Walkers may prefer to enjoy the sandy beach, following paths over the dunes or using board-walks between the dunes and built-up areas.

STAGE 3
Son Bou to Cala Galdana

Start	Son Bou
Finish	Cala Galdana
Distance	18km (11 miles)
Total Ascent/Descent	340m (1115ft)
Time	7hrs
Terrain	Easy at first along roads, tracks and clear paths through resorts, fields and woods. There are short steep ascents and descents later, in well-wooded valleys.
Refreshment	Bars and restaurants available in Son Bou, Sant Jaume Mediterrani, Sant Tomàs and Cala Galdana.
Public transport	Summer buses serve Son Bou, Sant Jaume Mediterrani, Sant Tomàs and Cala Galdana.

This stage starts in the twin resorts of Son Bou and Sant Jaume Mediterrani, and skirts an extensive marsh. After an easy coastal walk past Sant Tomàs, the route heads well inland, through elevated fields and across a series of rugged well-wooded valleys. It is possible to stay close to the coast, following a route covered on Walk 9. Towards the end of this stage, there is a splendid bay at Cala Mitjana, and even the built-up Cala Galdana is quite attractive.

Leave **Son Bou** by following the main road, Passeig Marítim, straight from a roundabout to the neighbouring **Sant Jaume Mediterrani**. ◄ The road rises gently, with a supermarket and restaurant down to the left, then continues on a level. At the end of the road is the Urbanización Torre Soli Nou. Turn left down the road, Calle Mare Nostrum, bending right and later offering views left of the extensive marshes of **Prat de Son Bou**.

This is also written locally in Spanish as San Jaime Mediterraneo.

The road keeps bending right, and climbs as if heading back into the resort. However, turn left down a broad road that soon ends, where GR223 markers will be seen at a gate. Follow a narrow track past level fields and cross a concrete bridge. Rise gently, turn left and go through a gate. ▸ Cross a dip and go through another gate to reach a farm building at **Son Benet**. Turn right down a narrower track, through a gate, then go gently downhill and turn left at a signpost. Some 220 stepping stones cross the marsh to reach a bridge and a gate, with reeds and yellow iris along the way.

There are good views of the marshes.

Turn left along a track at the foot of a well-wooded slope, bearing lots of tall pines. Go through a gate and turn left along a narrow path beside the edge of the reedy rushy marsh. Go through a gate and pass a little building, then go through gates and fields towards the low rocky point of **na Radona**, to reach a signpost. ▸

It is possible to reach this point directly from Son Bou, by walking along the sandy beach of Platges de Son Bou.

Turn right along the coast and cross a footbridge over a stone-built channel. Coastal grassland and narrow rocky inlets lie to the left, while a large field and the farm of **Atálitx** lie to the right. Pass scrub woodland, rocky islets and a more developed woodland, then some pines and juniper. Turn round a rocky headland to see a sandy bay and a resort. Stone steps lead to a concrete slipway, where a concrete road heads inland. ▸ Turn left as signposted to follow a broad, brick-paved, often tree-shaded path between sand dunes and buildings at **Sant Tomàs** (accommodation, shops, bars, restaurants, summer buses).

The beach can be followed instead of walking through Sant Tomàs.

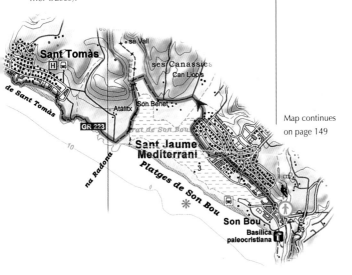

Map continues on page 149

147

Looking back along the sandy Platges de Son Bou from the rocky point of na Radona

Four board-walks cross the dunes between the resort and beach; otherwise the dunes are roped off for conservation. Pass a rocky point and keep walking to reach Camí de Cavalls mapboards at the mouth of a riverbed. This is normally dry, but has neat stepping stones. Go up to a road at the Bar Es Bruc. The road heading inland is flanked by an avenue of pines. Keep seawards of the bar to follow a well-trodden path overlooking limestone slab islets. ▶ Continue along the low cliff coast.

Note a curious structure by the path – an entrance to a Civil War bunker, with rifle-holes pointing across the path.

A soft sandy beach is reached at the **Platges de Binigaus**. Walk up through a gap in a wall to reach a signpost and shelter. At this point, the GR223 heads right and goes far inland, while a coastal track, linking with a rugged cliff path, heads left. ▶ Turn right to follow the GR223 along a track, with a slope of pines rising to the left and fields to the right. Reach a signpost at a staggered track/path junction, where there are water troughs on both sides of a wall. Walk 8 also passes this junction.

The cliff path is described in reverse in Walk 9.

Turn left up a rocky path. The path splits, left leading to a cave, and right omitting it, but both quickly rejoin. Zigzag up a densely wooded slope, then follow a wall down and uphill at **ses Pedreres**. Go through a gate and continue along the path beside a wall, falling, then rising away from it. ▶ The path levels out and is trodden down to limestone slabs.

The woods are mixed, with the tallest trees being pines and holm oaks.

Go through gates on either side of a walled track and pass a

Map continues on page 151

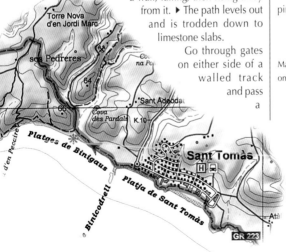

Paths and tracks are followed on either side of the Barranc de sa Torre

signpost, on which distances appear to be incorrect. Follow a gentle path through woods and pass a tiny stone shelter. Fences guard sheer drops into overgrown quarries. Go through a gate, turn right and walk down alongside a wall. The path becomes broad and is clearly old, with a drainage ditch alongside, in the **Barranc de sa Torre**. Go through a gap in a wall and climb a slope covered in dense pine forest. A steep stretch eases; the path goes through a gap in a wall and levels out. Go up a sort of rock-step, then

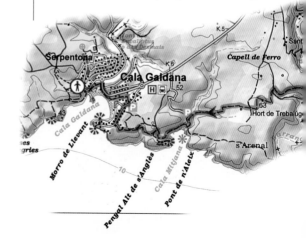

ascend gently. Swing right along a track on a broad forested crest, covered in pines and rock-rose. ▶ Go through a gate and follow the track onwards, passing through another gate at **s'Alzinar**. Turn left to follow a wall, climbing, meandering, falling and rising. The path is narrow but well-trodden and well-marked, eventually going through a gate to a track junction.

There is a glimpse of the hilltop farmhouse of Son Carabassa.

Walk straight ahead down a track, which is bendy and buttressed with stone on a steep and densely-wooded slope. Reach a gate and signpost at the bottom in the **Barranc de sa Cova**. Go through a gate and climb a zigzag path on a wooded slope. Go straight uphill beside a wall among tall pines, then gently down a terrace path overlooking the grassy sinuous valley floor. Go through a gate and down to the valley floor, crossing it from one gate to another, fording a stream in the middle if it is actually flowing.

Climb another densely-wooded slope and go through a gap in a wall, then climb further. ▶ The path levels out; then go through a gate and follow a wall onward among pines. Go through a gate for a short steep descent, then go through another gate to cross a track. Follow a narrow, rough and rocky path as marked, that climbs flanked by walls. Go through a gate and turn sharp right. Look left to spot a *barraca*, or stone-built cattle shed. The path rises and falls gently among pines, reaching a signpost. Turn left through two gates in a stone-walled enclosure. Follow a wall onwards through woods and turn right. Go

There are some particularly fine holm oaks beside the path.

151

Turn left to visit an attractive sandy beach flanked by limestone cliffs. Stone steps up to the left, marked by an arrow, indicate the cliff path to Sant Tomàs, used on Walk 9.

through a gate and note another barraca in a field to the left. Continue gently down the broad path, mostly in pine forest, through another gate. There is a little shed just to the left, and a sunken circle to the right.

The path swings left and right, drops more steeply. There are limestone outcrops and cliffs on the wooded slopes nearby.It suddenly climbs a little, passing through a gap between a cliff and a big boulder. Walk down to a gate, signpost, track and picnic site near **Cala Mitjana**. ◄

Head inland a little, take a track to the left of a car park, then turn left up board-walk steps, and turn left again along a terrace above the bay. The path rises and falls, and is cut into the rock on the way to a smaller rocky bay. There is a notice about quarries, and there are lots of square-cut blocks of stone arranged in piles. Follow a path up a wooded slope, past a cave house under a rock lip. Walk up a broad and bendy track, keeping left. Before reaching a gateway, turn left as marked along another track. Soon afterwards, turn right as marked down a broad woodland path. ◄

Note a limekiln to the left.

The path undulates and follows a stone wall through the woods. When houses come into view, turn right through a gateway, pass a mapboard and reach a road at a turning circle. Follow the road, Carrer Camí des Cavalls, a short way to a junction and turn right. ◄ Walk up the Avinguda de sa Punta, then go down past the Sol Gavilanes, to find a signpost on the left at a road junction. Walk down into a valley shaded by holm oaks, keeping left down to a beach beside the Sol Gavilanes.

Turning left is worthwhile, to reach a fine road-end viewpoint overlooking Cala Galdana.

Turn right along a promenade path, and note El Mirador Bar Restaurante on a limestone islet joined to the shore by a sandspit. Either walk to it and then cross a footbridge over a rocky inlet, or use a wooden footbridge below a road bridge and then follow wooden decking towards the mouth of the inlet at **Cala Galdana** (accommodation, shops, bars, restaurants, ATM, summer buses, taxis).

STAGE 4
Cala Galdana to Cala en Bosc

Start	Cala Galdana
Finish	Cala en Bosc
Distance	17km (10½ miles)
Total Ascent/Descent	220m (720ft)
Time	6hrs
Terrain	Mostly clear tracks and paths, sometimes along cliff coasts linking beaches, and sometimes further inland among woods. Some short steep ascents and descents until half-way, but gentler afterwards.
Refreshment	Bars and restaurants available in Cala Galdana and Cala en Bosc. Café at Cala Macarella.
Public transport	Summer buses serve Cala Galdana. Daily buses serve Cala en Bosc.

This stage has plenty of little beaches that are mostly sandy, but some may be blighted by piles of seaweed. The Camí de Cavalls does not always follow paths closest to the cliff coast, but some of these can be explored on Walk 11. There are a number of interesting Civil War bunkers and trenches, built to defend low-lying beaches from invasion. Apart from the resorts at the start and finish of this stage, there are no other settlements along the coast.

Leave **Cala Galdana** by walking along the Passeig Riu, towards the footbridge at the mouth of the rocky inlet. Climb stone steps, but don't cross the footbridge to the rocky islet. Pass a mapboard and signpost, climb a rocky path, pass leaning pines on the way round a headland and join a broad track. Turn left to follow it, rising and falling gently, often on bare limestone. There are pines, lentisc, heather, càrritx grass, rock-rose and asphodel alongside. ▶

Descend an amazingly convoluted flight of wooden steps, down past a café to a sandy beach hemmed in by limestone cliffs at **Cala Macarella**. Cyclists and horse-riders follow a parallel path to the right. Cross the beach

Paths on the left lead to viewpoints on the cliffs of ses Alegries, but return to the main path afterwards. The first and last of the four paths offer the best views.

The cliff-path heading left is explored in Walk 11.

and climb up a rocky slope of pines and bushes to reach a signpost, and turn right to follow the GR223. ◄ Climb from the bay, steeply at times, on a few log steps on a densely wooded slope. It is more open later, but still wooded, eventually levelling out at a signposted junction. Turn right, gently down and up through bushy scrub, then turn left, down through a gateway in a wall. Walk downhill, and down stone steps, then along the base of a cliff. Go up a bit, then down, joining a broad sandy path down to a junction and signpost. ◄

Turn left here for beach access at Cala Macarelleta.

Turn right up a broad path heading inland, with a cliff alongside to the left. There are pine trees all the way up the path, which becomes gentler later around **Marina d'Alparico**. Turn left at a signpost, still walking among pines as the path descends easily, though later it becomes lumpy underfoot where the bedrock pokes through. Pass a signboard for Cala Turqueta. Woods give way to lower scrub as the path broadens, still lumpy underfoot, down past a complex junction. The path goes through a gateway

Looking across the inlet of Cala Macarella to the tiny beach of Cala Macarelleta

154

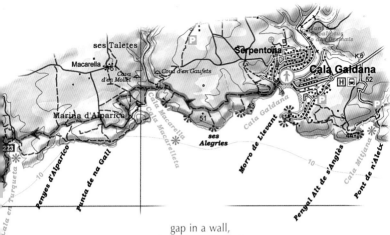

gap in a wall,
drops through woods
and reaches a sandy beach
flanked by cliffs at **Cala Turqueta**.
Walk to the head of the bay, where there are
lots of notices, and climb a few steps to continue.

A path follows a wall up a wooded slope with no
views. Go through a gate in a wall and continue through
woods. Go down and cross a path that offers access to
the coast, but keep ahead and climb instead. There are
some short but sometimes steep and rocky ascents and
descents, through bushy scrub to pass the mouth of the
bay. ▸ Cross a lumpy and awkward rocky platform at
Punta des Tambors, where vegetation is short and sits in
little hollows. Head back into the scrub on the way round
the next bay, reaching a signpost. Turn left along a path
that falls and rises, over and over, then turn right to reach
a mapboard near **Cala des Talaier**. ▸

Climb past the mapboard and turn left at a signpost,
following a path through a little gate and out of the scrub
onto a rocky platform. Turn round the headland of **Punta
des Governador**. ▸ An area of pine forest is roped off
from the rocky coast. The ropes, pines and rock all meet
the sandy beach of **Platges de Son Saura** at a signpost.

Walk along the beach, avoiding any deep piles of
seaweed. A line of sand dunes are roped off, and at the
far side of the bay a footbridge spans another rock trench.

Map continues
on page 157

There are views
inland to Monte Toro,
and ahead to distant
Mallorca.

Turn left to visit the
sandy beach flanked
by low cliffs.

Note trenches
cut into the rock,
and underground
structures, all
associated with the
Civil War.

155

Turn left along a track and follow it round a low rocky point covered in scrub woodland. Reach another sand and seaweed beach called Platja des Banyul, reaching a signpost. Go through a gateway in a wall and along a margin between rock and scrub woodland. Take short cuts across a series of small headlands, avoiding undercut edges, and note a monstrous boulder 'beach'. Go through another gateway in a wall and pass a big signboard for Cova dels Pardals. Cut across a headland bearing a drystone shelter.

Cross the rocky inlet of **Cala de Son Vell**, which may be stuffed full of seaweed. The path is flanked by bushes and leads onto another rocky platform, heading in and out of scrub before passing a signpost. Go through a gap in a wall; the path then follows a wall through more bushy scrub and across rocky areas. Go through yet another gap in a wall and continue, reaching a small white building at **Cova dels Pardals**. ◀

Stone steps lead underground into a remarkable cave leading into a rocky inlet.

Continue along the path, later going through a gap in a wall. The path becomes easier and passes another signboard for Cova dels Pardals. It becomes sandy underfoot on the way past a signpost, and the GR223 reaches **Son Xoriguer** (cafés, supermarket). Follow either the sandy beach and a stony path, or use a paved path a little further inland. Walk out onto the bushy point of **Punta de sa Guarda** and look out

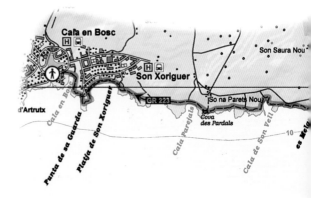

The sandy beach at Cala en Bosc

for more Civil War bunkers. Follow the shoreline, passing lots of juniper bushes, to reach a sandy beach at **Cala en Bosc**. Walk up to a road beside the big Hotel Cala'n Bosch, where there is a bus stop. ▸

Buses turn round at the nearby Parrilla Argentina, reached by following the road further inland.

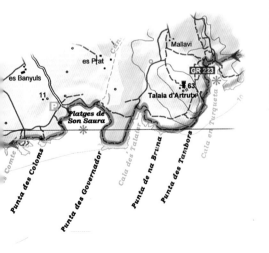

157

STAGE 5
Cala en Bosc to Ciutadella

Start	Cala en Bosc
Finish	Plaça dels Pins, Ciutadella
Distance	13km (8 miles)
Total Ascent/Descent	80m (260ft)
Time	5hrs
Terrain	Mostly easy on low-lying roads, tracks and paths. The walking is easy in built-up areas, but some other paths are very rough and rocky.
Refreshment	Plenty of choice in Ciutadella.
Public transport	Occasional buses link Cala en Bosc and Cala Blanca with Ciutadella.

This stage is fairly short and easy, though some of the paths cross rough and rocky areas. Some of the cliff scenery for the first half of this stage is impressive. Later, there are built-up resorts, mostly featuring scenic inlets, and a new port development, followed by the grand old city of Ciutadella, the former capital of Menorca. There should be plenty of time to explore the city centre after completing the walk.

Start at the Hotel Cala'n Bosch in **Cala en Bosc**, and follow the road straight to a footbridge with steps, and cross over a sea canal serving a small lagoon. Turn left to

The lighthouse, Farola d'Artrutx, at the south-western point of Cap d'Artrutx

Map continues
on page 160

reach the coast,
then turn right. The low cliffs and scrub are too rugged to take a path, so walk on the pavement beside the road, straight along the Paseo Marítimo. Pass houses and reach the prominent lighthouse of Es Far d'Artrutx, on **Cap d'Artrutx** (restaurant, bar).

A significant corner is turned here, and the Camí de Cavalls now heads northwards towards Ciutadella. Again, follow the road, with houses to the right, as the rock and scrub lying seawards has no path. ▶ When the road heads inland, turn left and follow a path to a mapboard beside a gate in a wall. Beyond this is a large signboard for Marina de Son Olivaret.

The path is clear, level and stony, through low flowery scrub. The path splits and the GR223 heads right, while the path to the left leads to a small stone shelter; however, both paths re-join later. A very gradual ascent reaches a Civil War emplacement and a signpost. Keep walking ahead as marked, and avoid a path heading inland, instead passing through a gap in a wall. ▶

Looking ahead distant resorts can be seen, and Mallorca might also be in view.

Maybe take a look over the cliff edge at Cala des Sac des Blat, but the cliff is seriously undercut and could collapse without warning.

159

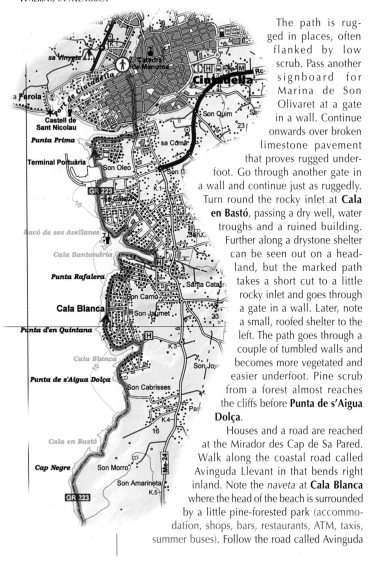

The path is rugged in places, often flanked by low scrub. Pass another signboard for Marina de Son Olivaret at a gate in a wall. Continue onwards over broken limestone pavement that proves rugged underfoot. Go through another gate in a wall and continue just as ruggedly. Turn round the rocky inlet at **Cala en Bastó**, passing a dry well, water troughs and a ruined building. Further along a drystone shelter can be seen out on a headland, but the marked path takes a short cut to a little rocky inlet and goes through a gate in a wall. Later, note a small, roofed shelter to the left. The path goes through a couple of tumbled walls and becomes more vegetated and easier underfoot. Pine scrub from a forest almost reaches the cliffs before **Punta de s'Aigua Dolça**.

Houses and a road are reached at the Mirador des Cap de Sa Pared. Walk along the coastal road called Avinguda Llevant in that bends right inland. Note the *naveta* at **Cala Blanca** where the head of the beach is surrounded by a little pine-forested park (accommodation, shops, bars, restaurants, ATM, taxis, summer buses). Follow the road called Avinguda de Cala Blanca round the inlet. ▸ Pass the Mirador Punta Rafalera, where a pub and restaurant face the sea.

Continue along the road, which later swings right and heads inland past a couple of bars and a supermarket. A short-cut might be spotted between the bars, where a concrete ramp leads to the rocky shore. Turn left along Carrer de sa Cadernera, and take the first left along Carrer des Tudó. This ends with a short path through a little gap leading to a signpost beside the rocky inlet of Es Clot de la Cera.

Turn right along a track, and watch for markers placed seawards of some houses. The track bends right and heads inland beside a long and narrow rocky inlet called **Cala Santandria**. ▸ Watch for the path heading inland a little, through scrub, avoiding the houses of La

There are places where it is possible to leave the road and walk along the cliff coast, but the rock underfoot is very rugged.

Note Civil War structures and, across the inlet, a sort of overhanging Martello tower.

Looking across the inlet of Cala Santandria to a fortification on a headland

Pascana and Tot Rustic on the coast. Continue along the track through pines and pass more houses. Turn left at a track junction and walk down the track called Carrer des Falciot, to reach a road. Turn left again down the road, which leads to a sandy beach at the head of the inlet. Actually, there are two beaches separated by a low rock outcrop. Keep left to leave the beach and climb a flight of steps carved from the limestone bedrock.

Keep straight ahead, along a bit of road above the Cova Sa Nacra snack bar. Walk along a short path as marked, onto another road. Turn left and follow the road round to the next little rocky inlet. Watch for a sign reading 'Baixada a Sa Caleta' and go down steps to cross the small sandy beach of Sa Caleta d'en Gorries. Climb steps to a road-end car park and turn left to follow a paved path, then a narrow path flanked by bushes, to reach rocky ground. Cross a scrap of sandy beach at the head of an inlet, and a rocky path becomes gravelly and easy as it follows a wall to a signpost and a road.

Turn left to follow the road, called Vorera dels Molls. ◀ Pass the new **Terminal Portuària**, or ferry terminal, where it can be busy whenever ferries berth. The road swings right as it is pushed inland by an inlet.

Turn left at a roundabout and the road crosses a sort of bridge over Canal Salat and its gentle valley, where there is a small sandy beach. Go through yet another roundabout and follow Carrer de Mallorca gently uphill into **Ciutadella** (full range of facilities). What looks like pine forest at the end of the road is the city square of Plaça dels Pins. ◀

Tamarisk bushes grow between the broad pavement and the rough coastal rock and boulders.

There are some bus stops on the far side, but buses to Maó and Migjorn are found by turning left for Plaça Menorca.

> The grand old city of **Ciutadella** was formerly the capital of Menorca, but under British rule Maó was deemed more suitable and has remained the capital ever since. Narrow, traffic-free pedestrian alleyways are paved with limestone blocks that are polished like marble. These allow the heart of the city to be explored, where visitors can marvel at the architecture, and are never short of food and drink no matter which way they go.

STAGE 6
Ciutadella to Cala Morell

Start	Plaça dels Pins, Ciutadella
Finish	Cala Morell
Distance	18km (11 miles)
Total Ascent	270m (885ft)
Total Descent	230m (755ft)
Time	7hrs 30min
Terrain	Easy at first through built-up areas, then some low hills and cliff coast where the ground is often rough and rocky, with some short, steep ascents and descents.
Refreshment	Plenty of choice in Ciutadella, Cala en Blanes and Calespiques. A couple of bar restaurants in Cala Morell.
Public transport	Regular daily buses serve Ciutadella and Cala en Blanes. Summer buses serve Cala Morell.

The Camí de Cavall seems to take the long way out of Ciutadella, but in the past the inlet penetrated further inland, whereas today it is spanned by a bridge. The popular resorts of Cala en Blanes and Calespiques have to be negotiated before the route heads into wild country. The cliffs are savage and there are low hills and little valleys to cross. The northern resort of Cala Morell is the last place with any facilities until distant Cala Tirant is reached.

Start on the Plaça dels Pins in **Ciutadella**. One corner of the square leads directly onto Plaça d'es Born, where there is a prominent central obelisk. Go to the edge overlooking the narrow inlet of **Port de Ciutadella**, and turn right to find a road leaving the square. The narrow Carrer de sa Muradet also includes a view over the inlet. ▶ The road runs along the top of the city wall, overlooking a valley and walled gardens. Pass the Museo Municipal de Ciutadella, which occupies a stout bastion.

A short-cut is available down a broad flight of steps, the Baixada Capllonch, then cross a bridge over the inlet.

Walk round the bastion and continue round the head of the valley, turning left at the Plaça de Dalt Els Penyals. Turn left again along Carrer de Santa Bárbara, reaching Plaça de Dalt Sa Quintana, where pines grow. Keep

Map continues
on page 166

There is a Camí de Cavalls mapboard in a car park nearby.

straight ahead along Camí de sa Farola, passing the old ferry terminal. ◄ Carry on along Camí de sa Farola, and catch a glimpse of a small marina to the left. The road runs down around a rocky inlet with a tiny sandy beach. Follow the road to a viewpoint at **sa Farola**, looking across the inlets to Ciutadella and Sant Nicolau. Walk past the *farola*, or lighthouse, and a chapel, or *ermita*.

A valley full of stout palm trees offers shade in a valley at the head of the beach.

A promenade cliff path runs parallel to a cycleway and a brick-paved road, where there is interesting low cliff scenery and possibly a distant view to Mallorca. A long rocky inlet pushes the road inland, but look for a signpost pointing down to the left. Go down stone steps on a short wooded slope, pass a cave-bar, then cross a sandy beach and walk up a road in front of a hotel at **Cala en Blanes**. ◄

Reach a complex junction where five other roads diverge. Signposts point to various bars, restaurants and shops, but follow the main road gently up through the resort. This is the Avinguda Simón de Olivar, fringed by palm trees. The road levels out at a supermarket and crosses a green space to pass The Black Horse, which offers home-made traditional British meals!

Go through a blue arch into the Urbanizació Los Delfines, also known as **Calespiques** (bars, restaurants, entertainments). The road descends gently to pass the Shopping Centre Es Forn, then turn right at a roundabout, signposted for the Ruta Pont d'en Gil. Follow the Avinguda Calespiques past Top Markets, then turn left,

A narrow rocky inlet leads to the resort of Cala en Blanes near Ciutadella

again signposted for the Ruta Pont d'en Gil, along the Avinguda des Pont d'en Gil. ▶ Pass a hotel and the 'CH€APE$T SHOP', eventually reaching the edge of the built-up resort.

The Camí de Cavalls goes through a gate near a cliff edge at **es Bancalot**; there are splendid views, not only of the cliffs, but also stretching across the sea to Mallorca. Keep well away from the cliffs, not so much following a path as walking on bare limestone. ▶ The path runs near a cliff edge, reaching a notice for Pont d'en Gil, where an arch can be seen in a headland, rather like a bridge. Another nearby headland, **Cap de Menorca**, is the westernmost part of the island.

Follow the path onwards and cross a small steep-sided valley, close to a rocky inlet. Climb a grassy slope to reach the walled Estacio de Bombament, or pumping station, where there is a road and signpost. Turn left along the road, which leads to a sewage works. Turn right and follow a wall up towards a prominent hill. Turn left as signposted through a gap in the wall, and the path is easy at first, then climbs steeply and rockily. Reach a fenced viewpoint at Sa Falconera. ▶

There is access down to the beach and cliffs at Calespiques.

Looking inland, there is a round stone tower.

The panorama embraces much of Menorca beyond Ciutadella and Monte Toro, as well as distant Mallorca.

165

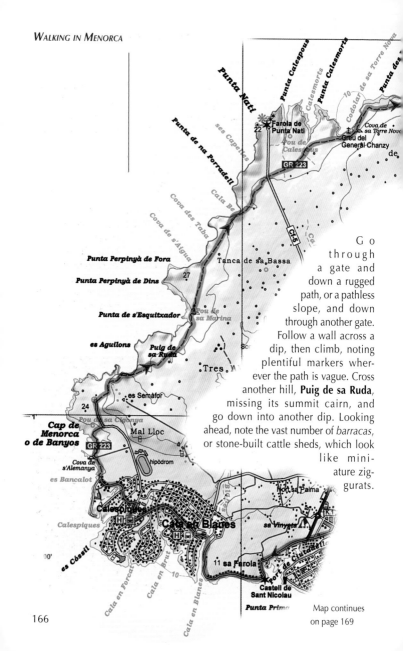

Go through a gate and down a rugged path, or a pathless slope, and down through another gate. Follow a wall across a dip, then climb, noting plentiful markers wherever the path is vague. Cross another hill, **Puig de sa Ruda**, missing its summit cairn, and go down into another dip. Looking ahead, note the vast number of *barracas*, or stone-built cattle sheds, which look like miniature ziggurats.

166

Map continues
on page 169

Molar den Bou
Punta de Son Esc
Punta de nd

Marina de Son Angladó
•93

arina
Escudero
Son Escudero

dA

On the ascent, pass one of these, flanked by walls with alcoves built into them. ▶

Go down through a gate in a wall, passing a signpost. Cross a dip and rise, then go down into another little valley and pass a well and stone troughs. Rise and pass another barraca, then continue across vegetated limestone pavement. Go through a gate in a wall and walk roughly on the level, but across rugged limestone pavement with less vegetation. Go through another gate in a wall and look left into the cliff-bound cove of **Cala Be**.

Marker posts keep well to the left of a well, troughs and a ruined shed. Follow the marked route to a gate and road, where there is a Camí de Cavalls mapboard. Either cross the road and go through another gate to continue, or turn left first to visit **Punta Nati** and its lighthouse. ▶

The GR223 runs alongside a wall, but later drifts away from it, running down into a dip, then climbing

Note thick masses of asphodel and limp bushes among the grass and limestone.

This detour is worthwhile for its cliff scenery, and to inspect two Civil War emplacements built in the shape of barracas, presumably for camouflage.

Looking over the cliffs into a rugged cove after crossing Puig de sa Ruda

Cliff scenery after Punta Nati, at Codolar de sa Torre Nova

again. The path is fairly easy, despite much exposed rock. Go through a gate in a wall and walk gently uphill, reaching a cliff edge overlooking the rocky cove of **Codolar de sa Torre Nova**. The path goes between two cairn shelters and passes a memorial cross and a cairn enclosing rusted iron from a steamship, the General Chanzy, that was wrecked nearby in 1910.

The path runs close to the cliff edge and later goes through a gate in a wall, continuing across rocky ground. There is one last view over the edge, before heading inland, across a little valley, and up through another gate in a wall. Follow a wall uphill, passing masses of pin-cushion plants, and head for a well and troughs. Go through a gap in a wall, noting another well to the right, and climb across rocky ground studded with more pin-cushions.

The path levels out among masses of asphodels, with juniper bushes dotted around, at **Marina de Son Angladó**. ▸ Go through a gate in a wall to see Cala Morell ahead, and the distant lighthouse at Cap de Cavalleria. Turn left, passing lots more juniper bushes, as well as low-lying lentisc bushes. Cross a gentle rise and go through a gate in a wall. Continue with a wall to the right and dense bushes to the left. The broad path drifts well away from the wall, then watch carefully for markers as there are other paths.

Eventually, swing right uphill, sometimes with another wall in view on the right, though mostly there are dense bushes on both sides. Go through a gate in a wall and continue up the path. Go through a gap in a wall and note a little stone shelter to the left. The path levels out and drifts left among asphodels and junipers. Walk over a crest and see hills in the distance, then head gently down and go through another gate in a wall. A track and a signpost are reached, so walk a short way down the track and go through a gate on the right, spotting a red-roofed hut marked 'Club Aeromodelisme Ciutadella'.

Turn right at a signpost and the path is

There is a last view back to Punta Nati and Mallorca.

169

flanked by dense low lentisc. There is a solitary white house away to the right, and a stone-built cattle shed to the left. The path follows a wall down towards the sea, all the way to a cliff edge, so don't forget to turn right! Walk down a path that is set back from the cliffs. ◄ When houses are reached, turn right inland, down alongside a wall, and go through a gate in a wall. Go further down alongside a wall, then turn left through a gate to reach a road and a Camí de Cavalls mapboard.

Enjoy views wherever it is safe to do so.

Turn right down the road, dropping steeply past peculiar white pillar lamps. Keep right to access an interesting series of caves. ◄ The **Coves de Cala Morell** are well worth exploring, but check the mapboard at the start so that nothing important is missed, and note that there are two paths that diverge, taking in different caves. One of these paths can be used to avoid a short road walk uphill, but in any case, continue up the road to finish this day's walk. When a junction is reached at the top end of **Cala Morell** (limited accommodation, couple of bar restaurants, summer bus services), the GR223 turns left along Via Lactia. ◄

Left leads to the beach of Platja de Cala Morell.

Via Lactia means Milky Way. All the road names are astronomical.

The little resort of Cala Morell is built around a rugged and complex cove.

STAGE 7
Cala Morell to els Alocs

Start	Cala Morell
Finish	els Alocs
Distance	15km (9½ miles)
Total Ascent	370m (1215ft)
Total Descent	400m (1310ft)
Time	7hrs
Terrain	Often well-wooded and hilly, passing fields in valleys and occasional beaches. A couple of bar restaurants at the start in Cala Morell, then nothing else.
Public transport	Summer buses serve Cala Morell. There is no other transport to any part of this stage. Taxis can be arranged to pick up at els Alocs.

Don't start this day's walk without having an 'exit plan', unless you are willing to start early, continue into the next day's walk and finish late at Cala Tirant. The northern coast of Menorca seems remote and rugged, lacking any useful facilities. Instead of bright limestone and white beaches, there is red sandstone and golden beaches, along with rugged, wooded and scrub-covered hills. Taxis can be arranged for pick-ups and drop-offs near the beach at els Alocs.

Follow the main road, Via Lactia, all the way through **Cala Morell**. ▸ Turn right at a roundabout where there is an arch, and walk along the road called Auriga, reaching a turning space and a cliff-edge viewpoint on the outskirts of the resort. Go through a gate to find a signpost, follow a wall inland and turn left. Low, dense bushy scrub includes juniper, lentisc, heather, a few dwarf fan palms and pines struggling to grow. Later, the pines are taller and the route passes the Aljub de Corniola, a tiled sloping square where rainfall drains into an underground cistern.

Follow the forested path onwards beside the wall, with occasional glimpses inland of fields and a substantial white farmhouse. The path descends gently alongside the

With time to spare, the beach area and the flights of steps serving it offer splendid views of nearby headlands.

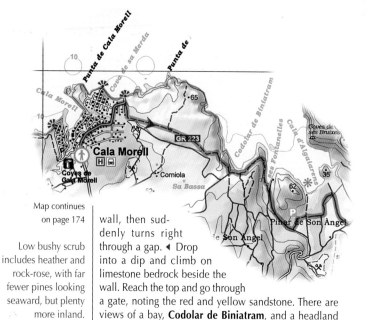

Map continues on page 174

Low bushy scrub includes heather and rock-rose, with far fewer pines looking seaward, but plenty more inland.

wall, then suddenly turns right through a gap. ◄ Drop into a dip and climb on limestone bedrock beside the wall. Reach the top and go through a gate, noting the red and yellow sandstone. There are views of a bay, **Codolar de Biniatram**, and a headland beyond it.

Red sandstone outcrops and boulders above Codolar de Biniatram

The path turns right, down to a track and signpost. Turn left along the sandy and cobbly track, gently downhill with views of bouldery cliffs and slopes leading down to a bouldery shore and boulder-filled sea. Climb on limestone, where sloping slabs drop towards the sea. Cross a gap and go down log steps on a rocky slope bearing pines. Pass interesting fishermen's huts tucked away among cliffs and huge boulders beside the inlet of **ses Fontanelles**. Note a Civil War structure here, then go up stone steps and head for a big concrete slipway at the head of the inlet. ▸

Despite the temptation to continue round the rocky shore, head inland along a track, passing hauled-out boats. Turn left through a gate and immediately right, heading inland on a sandy track flanked by trees and bushes. Walk gently up and down through pine forest at **Pinar de Son Angel**, where the dense understorey contains tall heather, arbutus and juniper. Turn left as signposted, walking gently down a broad winding track, with forest to the left and a field to the right. Enter a large walled car park and leave it at its lower end. Go straight across its access track to find a Camí de Cavalls mapboard. ▸

Leave the mapboard and walk gently down a broad sandy path beside fields, passing pines and particularly fine holm oaks. Reach a signposted junction and turn right. ▸ Follow a track from field to field, noting a solitary house to the right. Turn left as signposted at a track junction, walking through a field and crossing a humpbacked bridge over a reedy riverbed at **na Tombada**. Continue through fields and fork right at a junction, then when the track makes a sudden right turn, keep straight ahead as marked through a gate.

Climb a broad path up a slope of pines, go through a field and pass a cattle trough, then head down into woods. Go up through a cleared grassy space, into woods again, levelling out and then go down through a gate. Emerge from the woods at a signpost beside a field. Turn left and follow a path back into woods, undulating

Look into the water to spot lots of spiny sea urchins.

Turning left along a forest track leads to the sandy beach at Cala d'Algaiarens.

Or turn left here to reach the sandy beach.

through grassy areas in dense forest, possibly crossing a little stream if water is flowing near **Font de s'Hort Nou**.

There is a steeper climb through the forest, swinging right and down through a gate. Continue down through grassy spaces in the forest, now following a track. Go through a gate and down into an area of fields surrounded by forested hills, to a track junction and signpost. ◄ Turn left along another track, walk through a big field, rising through a gate into another field and then continue up through forest. Go down to a grassy area where **Font de sa Teula** lies to the left, spilling into cattle troughs.

Go through a gap and up a broad forest track worn to red sandstone bedrock. Pass a signpost on a forested gap, and walk down past tall pines and a few tall holm oaks, as well as arbutus and tall heather among the tangled lower scrub. It can be muddy at the bottom, and note a path on the left offering a short-cut; otherwise the broad path rises and falls a couple of times before turning left to follow a wall beside a narrow field at **Pla de Mar**. Cross a footbridge over a streambed and follow a wall, with long, narrow fields to the right and woods to the left. Later it is more open, and bushy scrub, largely of tamarisk, is passed on the way to the coast. Turn right to reach a signpost beside a bouldery beach at **Macar d'Alforinet**. Turn right again to follow a path staying inland of a storm beach, then climb a slope of red sandstone using log

There is a brief glimpse of a mansion.

steps. There is a drystone shelter to the left and a building to the right. A hole has been cut into the rock to the left, and the red trodden path goes up through a gate and passes above the building. Climb more log steps then follow a rocky or stony path over a slight gap. Rise and fall, past bushy scrub along the way to pine forest. Go through a gate and continue ahead as marked. ▶

A sandy path becomes rocky on the way downhill, and a stony path continues down through bushy scrub. Look left over a fenced cliff edge to see a sandy beach. Keep an eye on markers while walking down a soft path with loose sand, and avoid a maze of unmarked paths. Turn left when a signpost is reached above the golden beach at **Cala del Pilar**. ▶

The GR223 runs down through bushy scrub, past an information board and across rocks. When stepping down these rocks, look to spot a geological unconformity, where two different beds of sandstone join at the 'wrong' angle. Climb a rock step to reach a signpost standing on sandstone slabs. ▶ Turn right and climb steeply with the aid of log steps through bushy scrub. Walk down a stony path through bushes, then climb before reaching the next beach, which is bouldery and

A broad path rising on the right leads inland to a car park at Alzinar de Dalt.

To visit the beach, go down a flight of wooden steps on the left, on a crumbling red slope, returning to the path the same way.

A path on the left is prohibited, due to a landslide.

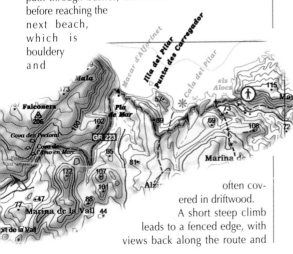

often covered in driftwood.

A short steep climb leads to a fenced edge, with views back along the route and

Soft red sandstone crumbles to form a golden beach at Cala del Pilar

Hopefully there will be the welcome sight of the pre-arranged transport!

ahead to the final bay of the day. Walk down to **els Alocs** and cross its pebbly beach. A little house lies inland, and a clear track runs further inland, flanked by lots of tamarisk bushes. This is far enough for one day, but there are no facilities whatsoever in this area. ◄

STAGE 8

els Alocs to Ses Salines

Start	els Alocs
Finish	Ses Salines
Distance	20km (12½ miles)
Total Ascent/Descent	650m (2130ft)
Time	10hrs
Terrain	A succession of rugged ascents and descents, sometimes short and steep, cross hills and pass little bays and beaches. Two river crossings are best avoided at high water or when stormy weather pushes the sea into them.
Refreshment	Nothing for the first part of the route. Bar restaurant at Binimel.là. Bar at the Ecomuseu de Cap de Cavalleria. Bar restaurants at Cala Tirant. Bar restaurants off-route at Fornells.
Public transport	There is no transport to els Alocs, though a taxi could be arranged for a drop-off. Summer buses serve Cala Tirant. Daily buses serve Ses Salines, for Fornells.

This stage along the north coast takes in small, but rugged scrub-covered hills, and a succession of bays and beaches. A couple of rivers have to be forded with care. Although there is no accommodation until the end of this stage, there are a couple of useful bar restaurants: one at Binimel.là, which could be used as a pick-up point for those walking all the way from Cala Morell; and the other at the interesting Ecomuseu de Cap de Cavalleria. There are Roman ruins to explore at Sa Nitja, and an opportunity at the end to move off-route to the lovely village of Fornells.

Starting at **els Alocs**, walk past the last building on the track, onto the beach. Turn right, then right again to head back inland. The GR223 runs parallel to the track, but is largely out of sight from it because of the tall vegetation in a streambed. ▶ Climb beside a wall on a scrub-covered slope, then go through a gap in the wall, climbing past càrritx grass and cistus towards pines.

Although the streambed can be crossed at a point further inland, it can be wet and muddy, so is best avoided.

Map continues
on page 180

Views ahead include
a series of islands,
headlands and the
lighthouse on Cap de
Cavalleria.

The rock type
changes from light
crumbly sandstone to
darker slate-like rock.

Go through a gate in
a wall and pass an animal shed,
then go through a gap in a wall and cross a gap between
hills. Walk down into a valley at **Marina des Mig**, where
the path is sometimes flanked by walls on both sides.
Climb straight up a steep path on a slope of càrritx and
cistus, following a wall over a hilltop. Cross a dip and
climb towards a higher hill, noting mineral veins in the
rock underfoot. The GR223 doesn't quite reach the summit, at 143m (469ft), but drifts left; however, it still the
highest point on the entire route. ◄

The path cuts across a slope that drops seawards,
and later there are high fields to the right, as well as a
barraca, or stone-built cattle shed. The path swings left
and descends towards the coast, but before reaching it,
swings right and misses a couple of little pebbly beaches
where driftwood accumulates. Cross a stream and climb
inland as marked. A short steep climb is followed by a
short descent to cross a little valley, then a longer climb
is followed by a descent to the attractive bay of **Cala en
Calderer**. ◄ Zigzag down to a couple of buildings and
look out from the sandy beach to the flanking cliffs, and
huge rocks poking out of the water.

Note a cliff-top cottage, but don't climb up to it. Ford
a stream on the sandy beach and head inland a little, to a
gate and cattle trough. (There is no further access inland
to Sant Jordi.) Turn left and climb a track as marked, then
before reaching the cottage, turn right up a path. There is
a good view of the bay before the path climbs and goes

through a gate in a wall. Turn right and climb beside the wall, then turn left to climb uphill from the wall. Pass a tumbled little ruin on a hilltop, then head downhill. Walk parallel to the rocky shore, but high above it, crossing easy-angled slabs of rock. Climb and level out on rock containing mineral veins. ▶

Huge boulders poke out of the sea at Cala en Calderer

There are views of islands ahead.

179

Walk down to the head of a rocky defile, which rather oddly leads inland, instead of towards the sea. Climb on red sandstone that is curiously dimpled and eroded. The path runs up and down on reddish and pale greenish rock slabs. Climb a steep vegetated slope, go through a gate in a wall and level out among càrritx and low, bushy mixed scrub. The path descends steep and stony, becoming convoluted, overlooking islands and a pebbly beach at **Cala Barril**.

A short track leads to a gate and a road. Turn left along the road, then right to leave it as marked. A path runs up through pine forest, through a gate on a gap, then down past a building and out of the forest. There are woods to the right and fields to the left. ◄ Fork right along a narrower path, then turn right along a dirt road, up and away from houses near **Cala Pregonda**. There is a short path down to the left, signposted 'hacia la playa', affording access to a golden sandy beach with a rocky islet and stack offshore.

A chapel-like building can be seen across one field.

Reach two gateways and go through the little one on the left. Turn right down a rocky then sandy path to the sandy beach. The path ends abruptly at a mass of weirdly-eroded red and yellow sandstone, so head inland. Spot a mapboard and pick up the marked path across a level reddish area where very little grows. A track rises and falls, cutting across a headland

Map continues on page 184

Sand, boulders, rugged islets and headlands at Cala Pregonda

to reach a pebbly beach where there is a patch of wetland inland. ▶ Walk up the path and through a gate, then down past a roped-off area and cross the sandy beach of **Platja de Binimel.là**. A river cuts across the beach; this must be forded on the beach, as it is too deep further inland. ▶

Come off the beach and follow a path beside a rocky shore. When the path climbs gently sloping rock, look left to see a small rock arch. Cross a small sandy beach hemmed in by low rock. Leave it, and watch for a marker, turning right uphill, left at a junction, then up to level gravel. Look across this to spot a marker to the left, then follow a narrow path, rugged underfoot past càrritx grass and heather. Climb until stony slopes are reached, bearing nothing but a few pin-cushion plants. ▶

Climb a stony path and go over a rocky crest, then down across a slope of càrritx and follow a wall downhill. Go through a gap in a corner and turn left, down towards a small sandy beach. Join a nearby track and turn left to follow it over a rise. Walk down, then along a rocky path, then follow another track beside a wall to reach a signpost. Turn left through a gate in the wall and cross a bit of sand at **Cala Mica**. The path rises between the sandy beach and a little building, then undulates past low and varied coastal scrub on rock. It becomes quite

Look out for a Civil War structure under a lip of rock.

A board-walk can be followed inland to the Bar Restaurante Binimel.là, a useful point to arrange a pick-up for anyone walking all the way from Cala Morell.

The lighthouse on Cap de Cavallaria can be seen ahead.

rugged past big boulders of crumbling sandstone, then climb to a noticeboard and go through a gate in a wall.

The path runs above the long, golden sandy beach of **Platja de Cavalleria**, then reaches a track where there is access to the beach. The sand ends at a jumble of big red sandstone boulders. Climb a long flight of wooden steps and turn right at the top. Walk up a broad stony path and go through a gap in a wall, then down to a car park and a road, where there is a signpost. Turn left along the road and cross a cattle grid. To the right of the road there are huge limestone boulders resting on red sandstone. The road later divides; keep left and watch for another signpost on the right, at the ruins of **Ciutat Romana de Sa Nitja**. ◀

The road leads to Cap de Cavalleria and its lighthouse, on the most northerly point of Menorca.

The Roman settlement of **Ciutat Romana de Sa Nitja** lies on both sides of the road. The square outlines of buildings are easily traced, despite juniper bushes dotted around the area. The nearby Ecomuseu de Cap de Cavalleria has a bar.

The GR223 follows a low wall away from the ruins. The path meanders through pine and juniper, gently rising and falling, so watch out for markers. Turn left as signposted for Cala Tirant, which is now in view, but distant. Walk down a track that is partly concrete, reaching a shelter above a little rocky cove. Walk up through a little gap, cross a little dip and then follow the path above rocks that slope to the shore, while lots of càrritx grass rises inland. Turn left downhill, cross a little valley, go up through a gate, along a fenced edge and down to a pebbly beach at **Macar Gran**. Walk straight uphill again and cross a slope, passing another fenced edge. Don't go down to a pebbly beach, but head right inland as marked, over a slight gap behind **Punta Negra**.

Go through a gap in a wall, where masses of càrritx grow on both sides. Walk down to join a broader path, which rises to a track. Go straight ahead as marked, up the track and across a broad gap swathed in càrritx. ◀ Reach a signposted junction with a broad dirt road serving houses at **Binidonairet**. Turn left down the dirt road, reaching

Monte Toro can be seen ahead inland.

The broad, golden sandy beach at Platja de Cavalleria

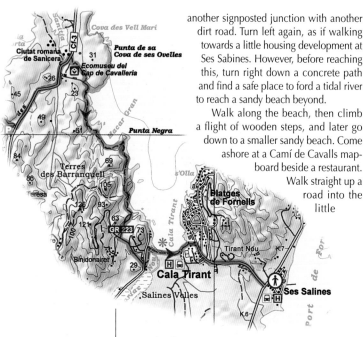

another signposted junction with another dirt road. Turn left again, as if walking towards a little housing development at Ses Sabines. However, before reaching this, turn right down a concrete path and find a safe place to ford a tidal river to reach a sandy beach beyond.

Walk along the beach, then climb a flight of wooden steps, and later go down to a smaller sandy beach. Come ashore at a Camí de Cavalls map-board beside a restaurant. Walk straight up a road into the little

resort of **Cala Tirant**, reaching a main road, summer bus stop and signpost. Turn right along the road, up past a supermarket, and out of the resort to a roundabout. Walk straight through and continue up the road. ◄ The road is flanked by pines, and a fine building to the left is called **Tirant Nou**. Walk down the road, through an arch, to a roundabout.

The Camí de Cavalls turns right along the Me-15 road at **Ses Salines** (accommodation, shop, restaurants, buses to Fornells and Maó). It is well worth following the Me-15 and its adjacent cycleway for 2km (1¼ miles) northwards to the delightful village of Fornells (accommodation, shops, bars, restaurants). ◄

There are lots of dragon trees at Es Antigons.

See Walk 14 for a circular route linking Fornells, Ses Salines and Cala Tirant.

STAGE 9

Ses Salines to Cap de Favàritx

Start	Ses Salines
Finish	Cap de Favàritx
Distance	24km (15 miles)
Total Ascent/Descent	430m (1410ft)
Time	8hrs 30min
Terrain	Roads and tracks through farmland and forest, then urban walking through resorts. Meandering paths and tracks through low hills, ending on a rocky peninsula.
Refreshment	Bars and restaurants at Ses Salines, Son Parc, Arenal d'en Castell and Addaia.
Public transport	Daily buses serve Ses Salines, for Fornells and Arenal d'en Castell. There is no transport to Cap de Favàritx, but a taxi pick-up can be arranged.

Roads and tracks provide an easy link between the resorts of Ses Salines and Arenal d'en Castell. Halfway along that stretch, an interesting ancient church site lies just off-route. There are scenic beaches, bays and inlets, with built-up resorts offering food and drink. Once the route enters the Parc Natural de s'Albufera des Grau there are only a few scattered farms, and no bus services. When the Camí de Cavalls reaches Favàritx, either a pick-up needs to be arranged, or the route has to be followed further to Es Grau.

Leave **Ses Salines** by following the Me-15 road in the direction of Maó. The road runs dead straight through a shallow rock cutting, passing fields and pine forest to reach a big roundabout. ▶ Turn left as signposted along the Me-7 road for Maó, and follow the cycleway alongside it. The road passes through pine forest, bending left and right. On the right-hand bend, turn left through a gate marked 'Salinas', where there is also a GR223 signpost.

Follow a track, soon leaving the forest. ▶ Keep right at a fork, crossing a concrete slab bridge over a murky creek. The track rises and falls gently past fields.

Not only do roads intersect here, but also cycleways.

Monte Toro can be seen to the right.

A track off to the right is signed to the **Basílica Paleocristiana d'es Cap des Port**. These extensive ancient church ruins are well worth inspecting, and there is a helpful noticeboard on site.

Return to the GR223 and continue along the track to the gateway of **Cap des Port**, where there is a signpost. Turn left across a stream, follow a path up through a gate, and rise along a track flanked by an avenue of tall pines. Reach another signpost and turn left up another track, walking through fields, into pine forest, and down past another signpost. Turn left, then further downhill, keep right at two junctions as marked, and pass a limekiln next to another junction. The track climbs gently through forest to yet another junction and signpost. Turn left and keep climbing, now with a wall to the right. The top of the low broad hill is free of forest, bearing masses of asphodels, crowned by a roofless ruined building.

Walk down the track and fork right along another track. Rise and fall gently, reaching the rushy, reedy edge of a wetland called **Prat de Son Saura**. It is difficult to see the extent of the water

Map continues on page 188

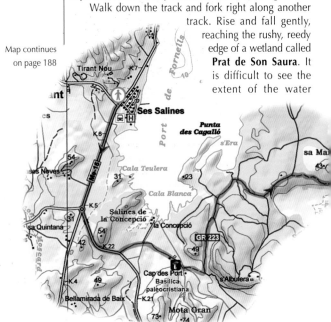

186

The rugged cliff coast between Son Parc and Arenal d'en Castell

from a low level, and when the path rises trees obscure the view, though distant Monte Toro is glimpsed. Follow the path past a sewage works, through a gate into a big gravel car park. The GR223 turns right and follows a dirt road out of the car park among pines. ▶

The dirt road joins another road, the Vial de l'Arenal, and turns left along it. Rise gently past a row of restaurants and a supermarket, reaching a road junction in **Son Parc**. Turn left along the road, or go into the adjacent little 'Parc Forestal' to avoid a stretch of road-walking, and continue up to another road junction. Turn right, then soon afterwards, turn left at yet another road junction. Keep right

Turn left through the car park to visit the nearby Bar Restaurant Es Bruc Nord. There is also access to nearby dunes, where a footbridge spans a river onto the white sandy beach of Arenal de Son Saura.

187

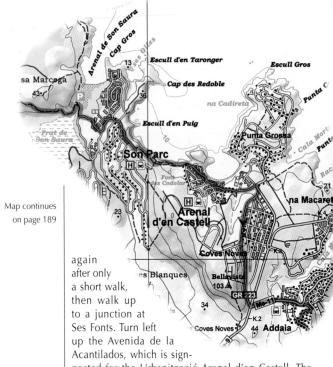

Map continues
on page 189

again
after only
a short walk,
then walk up
to a junction at
Ses Fonts. Turn left
up the Avenida de la
Acantilados, which is sign-
posted for the Urbanització Arenal d'en Castell. The
houses finish and the road continues into pine forest.

Turn left along a path through low scrub, and follow a rugged path with good views of limestone cliffs
between built-up areas. Reach houses, a Camí de Cavalls
mapboard, a road and a restaurant. Walk down the road,
and keep left down another short road that ends near a
very attractive sandy beach in a cove flanked by cliffs
at **Arenal d'en Castell** (accommodation, shops, bars,
restaurants, buses, taxis). Turn right and climb flights
of steps from the Plaça del Mar, passing shops in the
Poblado Marinero, reaching a signpost on the road called
Avinguda de s'Arenal.

Turn left along the road, past the bus stop and taxi
rank, eventually reaching a crossroads beside the Club-
Hotel Aguamarina. Turn right and quickly right again as
signposted up the Carrer de Savines, and continue all the

way up it. ▶ Just before reaching a roundabout, the broad paved Camí de sa Cornisa offers a view along the coast to Cap de Favàritx.

The left-hand side of the road is built-up, with a càrritx grass-covered slope to the right.

Walk straight through the roundabout as signposted, and down the road past pine trees, through an area in the process of being developed on the slopes of **Bellavista**. Follow the road up and down, reaching a crossroads with the busy Me-9 road that serves all the nearby resorts. Go straight down the Me-11 road, signposted through pine forest for Addaia. The road rises and runs straight ahead into the resort of **Addaia** (shops, bars, restaurants, summer buses).

Walk down the Avinguda Port de Addaia that passes a little pine-shaded valley and swings left. Turn right up Carrer des Tamarells. ▶ The road continues at Carrer Sant Llorenç, then turn left along Carrer Fontanelles. At the end of the road are three gates; go through the one in the middle. A broad concrete path flanked by walls leads to another gate. Go through it, turn left a short way up a track, then turn right

There is a fine view over the port and its marina.

Map continues on page 193

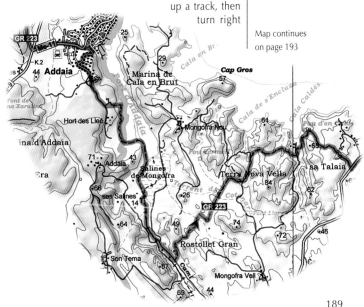

189

Looking along the narrow, built-up inlet of Port d'Addaia

through another gate and walk downhill. Pass through two more gates close together, pass a muddy patch trodden by cattle, then go up to a track and turn left up it. There is a forested slope to the right, and fields to the left, until the track levels out at a signposted junction.

Turn left through a gate, entering the extensive Parc Natural de s'Albufera des Grau (see Walk 16). Walk up the track, then go through a gate on the right and walk down a path to the shore of the narrow inlet of **Port d'Addaia**. Turn right to reach a boathouse, go through a gate and along a field path. ▶ Cross a footbridge, go through a gate, pass a cattle trough and turn left along a narrow grassy track. Pass another boathouse, where there is a view back to Addaia, before the track climbs through a crumbling rock cutting. Continue through a gate, reaching the head of the inlet, where the lagoon of **Salines de Mongofra** can be seen.

Tamarisk and other trees grow along the shore.

Turn a corner and pass a signpost, continuing with old saltpans to the right, bearing lots of samphire. The path later turns right, then left among pines. The next stretch of path crosses a level area that can get very muddy when wet. ▶ Eventually, the path wanders into woods, crosses a little footbridge and goes through a gate onto a track called **Camí d'Addaia**. Follow this track, and note how many rocky projections jut from rugged little sandstone hills to the right.

Red sandstone in this area breaks down to create lots of red mud.

Watch for a gate and signpost on the left. Turn left into woods, following a broad track with red sandstone poking through. Rise past pines with a dense, bushy understorey at **Rostollet Gran**. Cross a rocky gap and walk down into a grassy space. The path undulates through more grassy spaces, between dense bushy scrub, passing a waterhole and climbing through a gate. The path generally climbs through fields, crossing a couple of dips and a footbridge, then runs up through a gate. It becomes more rugged, rocky and stony, following a wall rising and falling across a bushy slope.

Join a track at **Terra Nova Vella** and turn left to follow it down through a valley where there are less bushes, but more càrritx grass, cistus and asphodel. There is a

Colourful euphorbia bushes along the ascent from Cala Caldés

glimpse of the sea and the track wanders down a valley towards it. A signpost points right up a narrow path, and the path rises and falls over and over again, crossing a wet and muddy patch. Turn left along a track, and while the GR223 goes through a gate on the right, ahead lies a little white house, and a *pou*, or well, that looks quite interesting. The track can be followed past tamarisk bushes to the nearby pebbly beach and rocky headlands around **Cala Caldés**, but if these are visited, retrace your steps afterwards.

Following the GR223 through the gate, climb a short steep slope using a few log steps. Limestone boulders litter the slope and masses of euphorbia bushes grow. Locate a breach in the limestone cliff and continue across a slope of càrritx to a ruined house. ◄ Turn right along a stony track, rising through càrritx and mixed scrub. It becomes sandy underfoot among pines, then grassy underfoot down through a gate. Pass through fields and go through a gate to reach a signpost and a road.

Views stretch back along the coast to nearby resorts and the distant Monte Toro.

Turn left to follow the road, crossing a cattle grid marked 'Son Chamil.la, propiedad privada'. However, the road downhill is public, flanked by low bushy scrub,

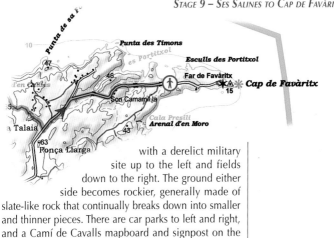

with a derelict military site up to the left and fields down to the right. The ground either side becomes rockier, generally made of slate-like rock that continually breaks down into smaller and thinner pieces. There are car parks to left and right, and a Camí de Cavalls mapboard and signpost on the right, beside a gate for Son Camamil.la, on the road to **Cap de Favàritx**. This is far enough for the day, but there is no transport, so a taxi pick-up needs to be arranged. Strong walkers, however, could continue walking to Es Grau.

Try to ensure that there is time available to explore **Cap de Favàritx** before leaving or continuing along the GR223. The road leads onwards to a striking lighthouse, where a black stripe spirals up the white structure. The vegetation in this exposed location is limited to cushion-like bushes and pin-cushion plants, plus the creeping fleshy fingers of mesembryanthemum. There is a roped-off pool, and a rugged sandstone headland to explore where the vegetation becomes more and more sparse.

STAGE 10

Cap de Favàritx to Maó

Start	Cap de Favàritx
Finish	Plaça d'Espanya, Maó
Distance	20km (12½ miles)
Total Ascent/Descent	490m (1610ft)
Time	7hrs 30min
Terrain	Tracks and paths vary from stony to sandy, close to the sea or a little further inland. Some areas are wooded and scrub-covered, and there are plenty of short ascents and descents among small hills.
Refreshment	None at the start. Bar restaurants at Es Grau and sa Mesquida. Plenty of choice in Maó.
Public transport	There is no transport to Cap de Favàritx, but a taxi drop-off can be arranged. Summer buses serve Es Grau. Plenty of buses serve Maó.

The final day's walk on the Camí de Cavalls runs partly along the coast, but mostly a little further inland. Low hills are often covered in scrub or woodland, and in the middle of the day the water and wetland of s'Albufera des Grau is a great distraction; however, save a detailed exploration of this area for another day, using Walk 16. When the route reaches the coastal village of sa Mesquida a short-cut road walk crosses a rugged peninsula, straight back to Maó. The 10-day circumnavigation of Menorca finishes back where it began in the city centre.

Start at a car park on the road to **Cap de Favàritx**, where there is a Camí de Cavalls mapboard. Go through the gate for **Son Camamil.la** as signposted, passing cushion-like bushes and stone-strewn areas. As the track climbs, stony spaces are enclosed by bushy scrub and there are plenty of euphorbias. Don't turn left, but climb over a rise, then turn left as marked and cross another rise. Head downhill and turn right at a junction, then go over a rocky crest and down again. ◄

There is a view of a reedy lagoon to the right.

The route passes a beach at **Platja d'en Tortuga**. Follow a roped-off sandy path, with a view back to Cap de Favàritx, then go down a stony cliff-edge path with a rustic fence alongside. Go down through a gate and choose whether to follow a roped-off path between the top of a pebbly beach and the start of some sand dunes,

A fisherman tries his luck from the pebbly beach at Platja d'en Tortuga

195

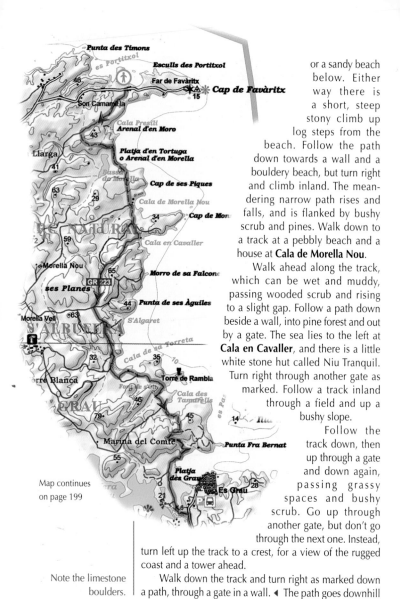

Punta des Timons

es Portitxol

Esculls des Portitxol

Far de Favàritx

Cap de Favàritx

48

Son Camamilla

Cala Presili

Arenal d'en Moro

43

Llarga

Platja d'en Tortuga
o Arenal d'en Morella

41

Bassa
de Morella

63

Cap de ses Piques

29

Cala de Morella Nou

34

Cap de Mor

RE NATURAL

59

Cala en Cavaller

Morella Nou

65

Morro de sa Falcone

GR 223

ses Planes

44

Punta de ses Àguiles

Morella Vell

63

S'Algaret

S'ALBUFERA

Cala de sa Torreta

32

35

orre Blanca

Fon ses sory

Torre de Rambla

46

GRAU

Cala des
Tamarells

79

45

es Par

14

Marina del Comte

Punta Fra Bernat

55

Platja
des Grau

Es Grau

28

21

K 6

P

Map continues
on page 199

Note the limestone
boulders.

or a sandy beach below. Either way there is a short, steep stony climb up log steps from the beach. Follow the path down towards a wall and a bouldery beach, but turn right and climb inland. The meandering narrow path rises and falls, and is flanked by bushy scrub and pines. Walk down to a track at a pebbly beach and a house at **Cala de Morella Nou**.

Walk ahead along the track, which can be wet and muddy, passing wooded scrub and rising to a slight gap. Follow a path down beside a wall, into pine forest and out by a gate. The sea lies to the left at **Cala en Cavaller**, and there is a little white stone hut called Niu Tranquil. Turn right through another gate as marked. Follow a track inland through a field and up a bushy slope.

Follow the track down, then up through a gate and down again, passing grassy spaces and bushy scrub. Go up through another gate, but don't go through the next one. Instead, turn left up the track to a crest, for a view of the rugged coast and a tower ahead.

Walk down the track and turn right as marked down a path, through a gate in a wall. ◄ The path goes downhill

196

again, eventually passing through a gate onto a beach that may be covered in seaweed at **Cala de sa Torreta**. There is a little white hut to the left, but the marked route turns right. Cross streams flowing into the sea to reach a track and a signpost. Follow the track through pine forest, then turn left out of the forest and climb past a solitary white house. ▶

All the rock around here is old, but there is a thin layer of much younger limestone on top of it.

Follow the path over a rise and down to the next little bay. Join a track and turn left to follow it, rising and falling. Note the **Torre de Rambla** off to the left. ▶ The track runs inland, rising gently, reaching a few pines and a signpost. Turn left up a sandy path, go through a gate in a wall, then walk down to a little beach flanked by rock at **Cala de Tamarells**.

Visit it if you wish, but the headland is very rocky and the tower itself is badly eroded and in danger of collapsing.

Shortly after leaving the far side of the beach, the path climbs inland, stony underfoot, with log steps. There is a view back to Cap de Favàritx, then Es Grau suddenly comes into view ahead. Walk down through pines, then rise and fall with another view of Es Grau. Walk down to the sandy beach of **Platja des Grau**, where there is a rocky islet that is linked to the beach by a sandspit. Walk along the beach a bit, but note that the GR223 heads inland. ▶

It is possible to walk all the way along the beach directly to Es Grau, but the GR223 doesn't actually go into the village.

Follow a roped-off sandy path inland, marked as 'itinerari 3', flanked by bushes. A well and cattle troughs

The heavily eroded Torre de Rambla must be close to collapse

197

are passed, plus information boards describing the natural surroundings. The path runs through tall pine forest, then leaves the forest after passing two boardwalk options for 'itinerari 3', which overlook the waters of **s'Albufera des Grau**. ◀ Cross a concrete bridge over water, and head for noticeboards, a Camí de Cavalls mapboard, a signpost, a gate and a road.

See Walks 15 & 16 for more details of nature trails in this area.

If food and drink are required, turn left and follow the green tarmac pedestrian strip beside the road to the little village of **Es Grau** (bar restaurants, supermarket, summer buses) only 400m distant. The GR223, however, turns right to follow the Me-5 road towards Maó. The bendy road is followed for 1km (½ mile) until a signpost points left through a gate. Walk along a walled path, through a gate and turn right up a field path. Go through another gate, turn right again to reach a signpost, almost back on the road. Turn left up through fields, noticing a hilltop farm, and go through a gate. Walk gently down a path flanked by bushes and cross a track made of crunchy shale.

Continue gently uphill as marked, past bushes, and go through a gap in a wall. Later, cross a track and follow an undulating path, and the sea comes into view. Pass a sign announcing the end of the Parc Natural de s'Albufera des Grau, at **Pla d'Enmig**, then descend steeply and suddenly. Go through a gate in a wall, up a bit, then down towards a white hide-away building on the rocky shore of **Caleta de Binillauti**. There is a signpost just before this point, marking a right turn across a valley and possibly a stream.

Climb and go through a gate beside a tumbled ruin, then go down bare sandstone slabs, passing lots of euphorbia among the bushes, as well as grassy spaces sprouting asphodels. The path undulates and the bushes give way to short grass and lots of pin-cushion plants. Walk down through a gate and pass another little white house on the beach at **Macar de Binillauti**. ◀ Cross the heaped, crescent-shaped pebbly storm beach, then climb and go through a gate in a wall. There is a notice warning of a military site inland, the Base Militar San

There are masses of tamarisk bushes and a series of small ponds inland.

Isidro; however, the GR223 climbs and follows the boundary wall encircling the base, and the base itself isn't in view.

Follow the path downhill and it broadens to become a track, dropping steeply through bushy scrub to a rocky and pebbly beach at **Raconada de sa Mesquida Vella**. Walk up the track and down to a gate, leading onto the military site, but turn left to find a GR223 gate in a wall. There are three options here: walk along the beach and climb a headland; head inland past a small lagoon to follow a roped-off sandy dune path; or walk along the sandy beach at **Cala Mesquida**. Whichever way is chosen, head for a white house and join a tarmac road. Follow this up through a long, linear car park and pass a signpost.

Follow a strip of red tarmac beside the road, down and uphill. ▶ Later the footway beside the narrow bendy road disappears, and the road crosses a bridge over a tidal creek. Walk up the road called Carrer Gran de sa Mesquida, into the village of **sa**

Note the Torre de sa Mesquida to the left.

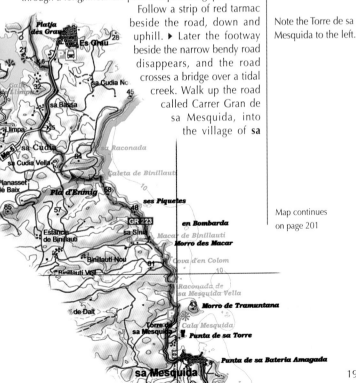

Map continues on page 201

A small whitewashed hide-away on the rocky shore of Caleta de Binillauti

Look to the left later to see a causeway footbridge leading to a house on a rocky islet.

From the top of the road Monte Toro can be seen in the distance, to the right of four wind turbines, and Maó is also in view ahead.

Three old buildings dominate the skyline; from right to left they are Sant Francesc, Sancta María and the Església del Carme.

Mesquida. ◄ Walk past the Bar sa Mesquida and a bus stop, then head uphill and inland to the right.

The road is the Carrer des Pa Gros, climbing a slope of bushy scrub and càrritx. Part-way up there is access on the left to the Restaurante Cap Roig; otherwise keep climbing. Keep right at a road junction further uphill, where left leads to Cala es Murtar. ◄ Walk down the road, still passing lots of bushy scrub, and keep right at another road junction, where left leads to Fortalesa de la Mola. Further down the road on the right is the access road for the Base Militar San Isidro.

The road descends more steeply and passes another junction. There is a Camí de Cavalls mapboard here, but the *usted está aquí* (you are here) marker is in the wrong place. Walk down and up the road, to be geeted by a view of Maó. ◄ Continue down past oil storage tanks and a power station, and cross over a busy road junction and continue towards Maó as signposted.

Cross a bridge over a river flowing into the head of the harbour of **Port de Maó**. The Marina Menorca is stuffed full of pleasure boats, and a broad pedestrian walkway passes it. Turn round head of harbour and walk alongside a busy

Map continues on
page 202

r o a d .
Watch for a
'Centre Ciutat' sign
pointing right, up Costa de ses Piques. The big building
at the top is partly the Museu de Menorca as well as the

*A house stands on
an islet just off-shore
from the village of sa
Mesquida*

The Mirador de ses Monges is worth a short detour to the left at the end of the road.

church of Sant Francesc. Turn left to pass it and continue by turning right along Carrer d'Isabel II. ◄ At the end turn right through the Plaça de la Constitució. After the church of Sancta María, turn left down the Portal de Mar and turn right into Plaça d'Espanya, to finish where the Camí de Cavalls started in the centre of **Maó**.

APPENDIX A

Route summary table

Walk/Stage No	Start	Finish	Distance	Time	Total Ascent	Total Descent	Page
1	Plaça d'Espanya, Maó	Plaça de S'Arraval Vella, Es Castell	8km (5 miles)	2hrs 30min	100m (330ft)	100m (330ft)	30
2	Plaça de S'Arraval Vella, Es Castell	Bar Via Maris, Alcalfar	8km (5 miles)	4hrs	110m (360ft)	110m (360ft)	34
3	Plaça d'Espanya, Maó	Plaça d'Espanya, Maó	15km (9½ miles)	5hrs	100m (330ft)	100m (330ft)	39
4	Sant Lluís	Sant Lluís	12km (7½ miles)	3hrs 30min	75m (245ft)	75m (245ft)	43
5	Església de Sant Gaietà, Llucmaçanes	Església de Sant Gaietà, Llucmaçanes	12km (7½ miles)	3hrs 30min	50m (165ft)	50m (165ft)	47
6	Airport	Sant Lluís	6km (3¾ miles)	2hrs	25m (80ft)	25m (80ft)	50
7	Plaça d'Espanya, Maó	Plaça d'en Mevis, Cala en Porter	23km (14¼ miles)	7hrs	200m (655ft)	200m (655ft)	54

Walk/Stage No	Start	Finish	Distance	Time	Total Ascent	Total Descent	Page
8	Es Migjorn Gran	Es Migjorn Gran	9km (5½ miles)	3hrs	130m (425ft)	130m (425ft)	62
9	Cala Galdana	Sant Tomàs	12km (7½ miles)	4hrs	300m (985ft)	300m (985ft)	66
10	Snack Bar Vimpi, Ferreries	Snack Bar Vimpi, Ferreries	12km (7½ miles) or 14km (8¾ miles)	3hrs 30min or 4hrs 30min	200 or 360m (655 or 1180ft)	200 or 360m (655 or 1180ft)	71
11	Cala Macarella or Cala Turqueta	Cala Macarella or Cala Turqueta	8km (5 miles)	3hrs	250m (820ft)	250m (820ft)	75
12	Ermita Sant Joan de Missa	Ermita Sant Joan de Missa	20km (12½ miles)	5hrs	100m (330ft)	100m (330ft)	79
13	Santa Àgueda	Alfurí de Dalt	11km (6½ miles)	3hrs	350m (1150ft)	400m (1310ft)	84
14	Harbour, Fornells	Harbour, Fornells	10km (6¼ miles)	3hrs	110m (360ft)	110m (360ft)	89
15	Es Grau	Es Grau	13km (8 miles)	4hrs	250m (820ft)	250m (820ft)	93

Walk/Stage No	Start	Finish	Distance	Time	Total Ascent	Total Descent	Page
16	Centre de Interpretació	Centre de Interpretació	6km (3¾ miles)	2hrs	150m (490ft)	150m (490ft)	97

Coast to Coast – Maó to Ciutadella

Walk/Stage No	Start	Finish	Distance	Time	Total Ascent	Total Descent	Page
Stage 1	Plaça d'Espanya, Maó	Bus station, Alaior	19km (12 miles)	6hrs	200m (655ft)	170m (555ft)	101
Stage 2	Carrer Joan Baptista de la Salle, Alaior	Carrer des Migjorn, Es Mercadal	16km (10 miles)	5hrs	400m (1310ft)	400m (1310ft)	108
Stage 3	Carrer des Migjorn, Es Mercadal	Snack Bar Vimpi, Ferreries	17km (10½ miles)	5hrs	260m (855ft)	230m (755ft)	113
Stage 4	Snack Bar Vimpi, Ferreries	Plaça dels Pins, Ciutadella	19km (12 miles)	6hrs	200m (655ft)	270m (885ft)	119

GR223 – Camí de Cavalls

Walk/Stage No	Start	Finish	Distance	Time	Total Ascent	Total Descent	Page
Stage 1	Plaça d'Espanya, Maó	Binissafúller	20km (12½ miles)	8hrs	210m (690ft)	210m (690ft)	131
Stage 2	Binissafúller	Son Bou	20km (12½ miles)	8hrs	210m (690ft)	210m (690ft)	138

205

Walk/ Stage No	Start	Finish	Distance	Time	Total Ascent	Total Descent	Page
Stage 3	Son Bou	Cala Galdana	18km (11 miles)	7hrs	340m (1115ft)	340m (1115ft)	146
Stage 4	Cala Galdana	Cala en Bosc	17km (10½ miles)	6hrs	220m (720ft)	220m (720ft)	153
Stage 5	Cala en Bosc	Plaça dels Pins, Ciutadella	13km (8 miles)	5hrs	80m (260ft)	80m (260ft)	158
Stage 6	Plaça dels Pins, Ciutadella	Cala Morell	18km (11 miles)	7hrs 30min	270m (885ft)	230m (755ft)	63
Stage 7	Cala Morell	els Alocs	15km (9½ miles)	7hrs	370m (1215ft)	400m (1310ft)	171
Stage 8	els Alocs	Ses Salines/Fornells	20km (12½ miles)	10hrs	650m (2130ft)	650m (2130ft)	177
Stage 9	Ses Salines	Cap de Favàritx	24km (15 miles)	8hrs 30min	430m (1410ft)	430m (1410ft)	185
Stage 10	Cap de Favàritx	Plaça d'Espanya, Maó	20km (12½ miles)	7hrs 30min	490m (1610ft)	490m (1610ft)	194

APPENDIX B
Language notes

There are two official languages in Menorca: Castilian Spanish and Catalan. Catalan is spoken from Andorra to València, as well as on the Balearic Islands. Menorquí is a dialect of Catalan and includes words of French and Arabic origin. No-one expects visitors to speak Catalan, let alone Menorquí, and any Spanish you may learn is readily understood on Menorca. Many people in the resorts and hotels speak English, German and other languages but this may not be so in small villages and in the countryside.

Catalan in its written form may be understood by anyone with a reasonable knowledge of Spanish, but the spoken language is another matter. Most islanders speak Menorquí between themselves, so conversations on buses and in bars and shops may be incomprehensible to visitors. However, if you speak even a little Spanish you will find that people are delighted and will help you all they can, and even more so if you attempt to converse in Catalan. It is well worth taking the trouble to learn a few words and phrases so as to be able to pass the time of day with local people.

Spanish is pronounced more or less exactly as it is spelt, according to certain rules, so a reasonable attempt at pronunciation can be made. Unless there is an accent to denote emphasis, the accented syllable in a word depends on the last letter of the word: if it ends in an n, s or a vowel, the accent is on the penultimate syllable; if the last letter is anything else it is on the last syllable. There are plenty of English–Spanish phrasebooks on the market, and you should make every effort to use the language. Opportunities for English speakers to learn Catalan are limited, but the book, CD or Kindle version of *Complete Catalan* is a good place to start.

Key to Spanish pronunciation
The following guide is given for reference and is no substitute for listening to people talking on audio courses, radio, television or, best of all, in real life.

a between a in lass and in father – *adiós* – goodbye
b as in English – *banco* – bank
c used before i and e, like th in thin – *cinco* – (thinco) five
c before anything else, as in cat – *cliente* – customer
ch as in church – *chico* – boy
d used at beginning of word, like d in dog – *dos* – two
d in other places, like th in though – *verdad* – true
e as in men, but at end of word as in day – *leche* – milk
f as in English – *fácil* – easy
g used before a,o,u, or consonants, as in gas – *gasolina* – petrol
g before e and i as ch in loch – *gente* – people
gu used before a, like gw – *agua* – (agwa) water
h is always silent – *hombre* – (ombre) man
i as in machine – *litro* – litre
j like ch in loch – *ajo* – garlic

k as in English – *kilo* – kilo
l as in English – *libro* – book
ll like lli in million – *me llamo* – I'm called
m as in English – *mantequilla* – butter
n as in English – *naranja* – orange
ñ as ni in onion – *los niños* – the children
o between top and for – *oficina* – office
p as in English – *pan* – bread
q like English k – *quizás* – perhaps
r pronounced slightly rolled – *el norte* – the north
rr pronounced strongly rolled – *carretera* – main road
t as in English – *tienda* – shop
u as in boot – *usted* – you (polite form)
v like a soft English b – *vaso* – (baso) glass
x used at end of word, like tch – Artrutx (placename)
x used between vowels, like gs – *taxi* – (tagsi) taxi
y like y in yes – *mayor* – main
y the word y, as the i in machine – *y* – and
z as th in thick – *manzana* – (manthana) apple

Key to Catalan pronunciation
The sounds are broadly the same as for Spanish, including those pronounced as in English, but with a few notable exceptions. Mastering the rules ensures you will have no trouble with placenames.
c used before e or i is soft, otherwise hard, never lisped – *cinc* – (sink) five
ç sounds like ss as in English – *plaça* – (plassa) square
g used before e or i is soft, otherwise hard
j is pronounced soft the same as the French pronounce Jean
ll like lli in million
l.l sounds like ll as in English, as in – *col.laboració* – collaboration
ny is always used in Catalan where Spanish uses ñ – *senyora/señora*
qu used before e or i is like k, but before a or o is like kw
r is pronounced rolled at the start of a word
v used at the start of a word sounds like b; otherwise sounds like f
z is pronounced like an English z and is never lisped

Basic words and phrases
Some very basic words and phrases are included here because it can be useful to have reference to them without carrying a separate phrase book in your rucksack. Note: An upside down question mark or exclamation mark is always used at the beginning of a question or exclamation in Spanish.

English	Spanish	Catalan

Basic greetings and niceties

English	Spanish	Catalan
hello	holá	hola
good morning	buenos días	bon dia
good afternoon	buenas tardes	bones tardes
goodnight	buenas noches	bona nit
goodbye	adiós	adéu
see you tomorrow	hasta mañana	fins demà
see you later	hasta luego	fins després
yes/no	sí/no	si/no
please	por favor	per favor
thank you	gracias	gràcies
that's all right	de nada	de res
thank you very much	muchas gracias	moltes gràcies
excuse me	perdón	perdoni
I'm sorry	lo siento	ho sento

When you are struggling

English	Spanish	Catalan
I'm English (man)	soy inglés	sóc anglès
I'm English (woman)	soy inglesa	sóc anglesa
I don't understand	no comprendo	no ho entenc
would you repeat please?	¿puede repetir, por favor?	ho pot repetir, per favor?
more slowly, please	más despacio, por favor	mès lent, per favor
what did you say?	¿qué ha dicho?	que m'ha dit?
what is that?	¿qué significa ésto?	què vol dir això?
do you speak English?	¿habla inglés?	parla anglès?
I don't speak Spanish	no hablo español	no parlo espanyol
I don't speak Catalan	no hablo catalán	no parlo català

Directions around town

English	Spanish	Catalan
there is/are, is/are there	hay	hi ha
is there a bank near here?	¿hay un banco por aquí?	hi ha un banc prop d'aquí?
where is...?	¿dónde está...?	a on és...?
...the post office?	¿...la oficina de correos? ...	l'oficina de correus?
...the toilet?	¿... los servicios?	...el banyo?
men	señores/hombres/	caballeros homes
women	señoras/mujeres/	dones
open/closed	abierto/cerrado	obert/tancat
today/tomorrow	hoy/mañana	avui/demà

English	Spanish	Catalan
next week	la semana que viene	la setmana que ve
where can one buy...?	¿dónde se puede comprar...?	a on se pot comprar?...
a newspaper/stamps	un periódico/sellos	un diari/segells
I'd like that	quería eso	voldria OK
I'll have this	me llevo ésto	m'en duc aixó
how much?	¿cuánto cuesta?	quant val?

A room for the night

do you have a room?	¿tiene una habitación?	té alguna habitació?
double/single	doble/individual	doble/individual
tonight	esta noche	aquesta nit
for two/three nights	para dos/tres noches	per dues/tres nits
how much is the room?	¿cuanto cuesta la habitación?	quan val l'habitació?
with bath/without bath	con baño/sin baño	amb bany/sense bany

Eating and drinking (also see Food)

drinks	bebidas	begudes
breakfast	desayuno	berenar
lunch/dinner	almuerza/cena	dinar/sopar
I'd like/we'd like	quiero/queremos	voldria/voldriem
I'll have/we'll have	tomo/tomamos	prendré/prendrema
black coffee	un café solo	un café sol
two black coffees	dos cafés solos	dos cafés sols
white coffee	un café con leche	un café amb llet
three white coffees	tres cafés con leches	tres cafés amb llet
tea with milk	un té con leche	un tè amb llet
tea with lemon for me	un té con limón para mi	un tè amb llimona
beer	una cerveza	una cervesa
the house wine	el vino de la casa	el vi de la casa
a glass of red wine	un vaso de vino tinto	un tassó de vi negre
white wine	vino blanco	vi blanca
dry sherry	un jeréz seco	un xerès seca
bottle of water	una botella de agua	una botella d'aigo
fizzy/still	con gas/sin gas	amb gas/sense gas
orange juice	zumo de naranja	suc de taronja
starters	prima plato primer	plat
soup	sopa	sopa
eggs, egg dishes	huevos	ous
fish, fish dishes	pescados	peix

English	Spanish	Catalan
seafood/shellfish	mariscos	marisc
meat, meat dishes	carne	carn
game	carne de caza	carn de caça
vegetables	verduras/legumbres	verdures/llegums
I'm vegetarian	soy vegetariano	sóc vegetarià
cheese	queso	formatge
fruit	fruta	fruita
ice-cream	helado	gelat
desserts	postres	postres
sandwich	bocadillo	panet
anything else?	¿algo más?	qualque cosa més?
nothing, thank you	nada más, gracias	res més, graciès
the bill, please	la cuenta, por favor	el compte, per favor
packed lunches	picnics	picnics
two packed lunches	dos picnics	dos picnics
for tomorrow	para mañana	per demà

Getting around Menorca

by car/on foot	en coche/a pie	en cotxe/a peu
how do I get to Maó?	¿por dónde se va a Mahón?	com es va a Maó?
where is...?	¿dónde está...?	a on és...?...
the bus station?	¿...la estación de autobúses? ...	l'estació d'autobusos?...
the bus stop?	¿...la parada de autobús?	...la parada d'autobús?...
for Ciutadella?	¿...para Ciutadella?	...per Ciutadella?
how much is the fare?	¿cuánto vale el billete?	quan val el bitllet?
return	ida y vuelta	d'anada i tornada
single	solamente ida	només anada

Directions for walkers

where is the footpath to...?	¿dónde está el camino a...?	a on és el camí a...?
may we go this way?	¿se puede pasar por aquí?	se pot passar per aquí?
is it far?	¿está lejos?	està lluny?
how far?	¿a qué distancia?	a quina distància?
how long?	¿cuánto tiempo?	a quans minuts?
very near?	¿muy cerca?	molt proper?
left/right	izquierda/derecha	a l'esquerra/a la dreta
straight on	todo recto	tot recte
first left	la primera a la izquierda	la primera a l'esquerra
second right	la segunda a la derecha	la segona a la dreta

English	Spanish	Catalan
in front of the church	delante de la iglesia	davant l'església
behind the hotel	detrás del hotel	darrera l'hotel
at the end of the street	al final de la calle	al final del carrer
after the bridge	después del puente	passat el pont
where are you going?	¿adónde va/van?	a on va/van?
I'm going/we're going to...	voy a/vamos...	vaig a/anam a...
a right of way	derecho de paso	dret de pas
please close	cierre, por favor	tancau, per favor
dogs on guard	cuidado con el perro	alerta amb el ca

Days of the week

Monday	lunes	dilluns
Tuesday	martes	dimarts
Wednesday	miércoles	dimecres
Thursday	jueves	dijous
Friday	viernes	divendres
Saturday	sábado	dissabte
Sunday	domingo	diumenge

Emergencies

Help! Fire!	¡Socorro! ¡Fuego!	Ajuda! Foc!
Police	Policía/Guardia Civil	Policía/Guardia Civil
there's been an accident	ha habido un accidente	hi ha hagut un accident
call a doctor quickly	llame a un medico, rapidamente	cridin al metge, ràpidament
it's urgent!	¡es urgente!	és urgent!

Food

Menorquín cuisine, or cuina Menorquina, is not always similar to that of Catalonia on the mainland. Fish dishes are a speciality and so are tapas, served with drinks in many bars. They are usually behind glass on the counter and you can point to the ones you want. Small or large helpings are offered and a large one can make a substantial meal. Meals in hotels may involve table service or a self-service buffet with an excellent selection. The following is a brief list, and dishes can become complex as Menorcans are adept at cooking mil formes, or 'a thousand ways'.

Angules	small eels fried whole in batter
Arroz de la terra	similar to couscous
Bacallà	dried salted codfish, often served in casseroles
Brossat menorquí	Menorcan curd pudding
Butifarró blanc/negre	white/black Catalan spiced sausage

Calamars	squid, served a la romana or deep fried, in rings
Caldereta de peix	fish soup with rice and slices of bread
Cargols	snails cooked in garlic mayonnaise sauce
Coca bamba	a potato cake often eaten with hot chocolate
Embotits	sausages, generally made of pork, ranging from white to black
Ensaimada	a light, flaky spiral bun sprinkled with icing sugar
Escopinyes al forn	baked clams covered in breadcrumbs
Flaons menorquins	pastries stuffed with savoury cheese mixes
Formatge	cheese, generally sold at three stages of maturity
Frit menorquía	fry-up containing lamb or pork
Gambes	prawns
Greixera	pressed cold meats with egg, artichokes, peas, beans and herbs
Guisantes a la catalana	peas fried with ham and onions
Laccao/Saccao	trade names for a hot or cold chocolate drink like cocoa
Llagosta	lobster, traditionally with onions, tomatoes, garlic and parsley
Macarrons amb grevi	macaroni with chopped or ground meat in sauce
Maionesa	mayonnaise, said to have been invented in Mahón (Maó)
Musclos a la marinera	mussels cooked in a spicy sauce
Napolitanas	like sausage rolls but filled with chocolate or custard (crema)
Oli d'oliva	olive oil, used extensively for cooking and dressing
Paella	cooked to order for a minimum of two people and take at least half an hour, combining rice with various seafoods, meat and vegetables
Paella catalana	spicy sausage, pork, squid, tomato, chilli pepper and peas
Paella marinera	fish and seafood only
Panada (Empanada)	meat and/or vegetable pie
Perol	layers of chopped potatoes, tomatoes, herbs and spices, rolled in breadcrumbs and baked
Sobrasada	pork-liver sausage, bright red with pimento
Truita	can mean trout or omelette in Menorquí, hence:
Truita a la navarra	trout stuffed with bacon or smoked ham
Truita de patates (Tortilla española)	omelette with potatoes
Xocolata calenta (Chocolate a la taza)	thick hot chocolate for dipping pastries such as ensaimadas
Xoriç (chorizo)	a strong spicy sausage
Xoriguer	brand name of Menorcan gin

Place names

Most places in Menorca had two names in the past, Spanish and Menorquí. Since Menorquí was given co-equal status with Spanish, almost all Spanish placenames have vanished from signposts and street signs. In fact, only in a few tourist places are there any Spanish signs, and Menorquí may be the only language in evidence in rural areas.

Confusion is likely to arise if you use old maps and guidebooks, which generally show only Spanish placenames. The new Alpina map uses only Menorquí placenames. Names are fairly similar as a rule, but some hotels and businesses insist on using Spanish forms for their addresses, so you may find a hotel listed as being in Mahón, but you will have to follow road signs for Maó to get there!

Some placename pronunciations

Artrutx	are-trutch
Binissafúller	bini-sa-foo-ye
Ciutadella	see-oo-ta-day-a
Llucmaçanes	l'yook-ma-sa-nes
Maó	ma-oh
Menorca	men-orka
Puig	pooj (with a soft j)

APPENDIX C
Topographical glossary

This glossary is given in Catalan and English only, to assist walkers who are interested in placenames to be able to unravel their meanings. The list contains names that occur regularly on maps and throughout this guide. Some names seen frequently on signs are also included. (Where some Spanish placenames may still be lingering, these are shown in brackets.)

albufera	lagoon	*cocó/cocons*	very small rock pool/s
aljub	small underground reservoir	*coll*	mountain pass
alzina	evergreen oak	*coma*	valley
aguila	eagle	*comellar*	small valley
arena	sand	*comuna*	communal land
avenc	deep cleft	*corral*	animal pen
avinguda (avenida)	avenue	*costa*	coast
badia	bay	*cova/coves*	cave/caves
baix	low	*dalt*	high
barraca	stone cattle shed	*des/d'es*	of the
bassa	small pool	*ermita*	hermitage
barranc	ravine	*es*	the
bini	house of (Arabic)	*església*	church
blanca	white	*far*	lighthouse
bosc	woodland	*font*	spring/fountain
cala	small bay or cove	*forn de calç*	limekiln
caleta	small bay	*gran*	big
camí	path	*illa/illes*	island/s
camp	field	*jardí*	garden
cap	rocky point	*llarga*	long
capella	chapel	*major*	main/big
carrer (calle)	street	*mar*	sea
cas/casa	house	*marge*	drystone-walled buttress
caseta	small house/hut		
castell	castle	*migdia*	midday
cavall	horse	*mirador*	viewpoint
cingle	cliff	*molí*	mill
clot	hollow/depression	*moro*	moor (arab)

museu	museum	*roca*	rock
palau	palace	*roig*	red
parc	park	*santuari*	sanctuary
pinar/pins	pine	*sant/santa*	male/female saint
pla	plain/flat land	*talaia*	watch tower
plaça (plaza)	square	*taula*	t-shaped monument
platja (playa)	beach		
pont	bridge	*torre*	tower
port (puerto)	port or harbour	*torrent*	river
porta	door	*vall*	valley
pou	well	*vell*	old
puig	hill or mountain	*vent*	wind
pujol	hill	*verd*	green
punta	rocky point	*verger*	fertile area
rei	king	*vinyes*	vineyard

APPENDIX D
Useful contacts

Government
Consell Insular de Menorca
Plaça Biosfera 5, 07703 Maó
tel 971 356050
www.cime.es

Flights to Menorca
To check the abundant facilities available on arrival at the airport, visit the following website, select 'Menorca' and set the language to 'English'.
www.aena.es

Airlines serving Menorca include, but are not limited to, the following:

Jet2, www.jet2.com

Monarch, www.monarch.co.uk

Ryanair, www.ryanair.com

Iberia, www.iberia.com

Spanair, www.spanair.com

Vuelair, www.vuelair.com

Ferries to Menorca
Ferries operate both from mainland Spain and neighbouring Mallorca.

Baleària, www.balearia.com, Alcúdia and Barcelona to Ciutadella

Iscomar, www.iscomar.com, Alcúdia to Ciutadella

Acciona Trasmediterránea, www.trasmediterranea.es, Barcelona, Valencia and Palma to Maó

General Menorca Tourism
Fundació Destí Menorca, tel 902-929015, www.menorca.es

Tourist information offices
Airport Arrivals Hall, tel 971-157115

Plaça de S'Esplanada, Maó
tel 971-367415

Moll de Levant, Port de Maó
tel 971-355952

Plaça de la Catedral, Ciutadella
tel 971-382693

Casa del Contramaestre, Fornells
tel 971-158430

Public transport
There are three main bus companies, operating full summer timetables and reduced winter timetables. Note that there are express and stopping services along the busy main road between Maó and Ciutadella. Use the express to travel quickly between the two cities, but use the stopping service to get on or off at any of the towns in-between. The local newspaper, *Menorca Diario Insular*, publishes up-to-date timetables on its Transportes Autobuses page. Alternatively, copy timetables at the bus station in Maó, ask for timetables at tourist information offices or download them from the following websites:

Transportes Menorca (TMSA), www.transportesmenorca.net – Maó to Ciutadella and most settlements and resorts south of the main road.
Torres, www.e-torres.net – Airport service to and from Maó; city services around Maó; all the west coast resorts from Ciutadella.

Autos Fornells, www.autosfornells.com – Fornells to Maó, Es Mercadal, and many settlements in north-east Menorca.

GR223 – Camí de Cavalls

Websites
Official website for the route
www.elcamidecavalls.cat/cami

Jaume Tort's GR223 website
www.gr223.info

Maps
1:50,000 Editorial Alpina Map of Menorca

Extracts from the Editorial Alpina map, www.editorialalpina.com, are used throughout this guidebook. A copy of the full map allows walkers to see where all the featured walking routes lie in relation to each other, and this is widely available from outlets around Menorca. The map can be obtained in advance from UK stockists:

Stanfords
12-14 Long Acre
London
WC2E 9BR
tel 0207 8361321
www.stanfords.co.uk

The Map Shop
15 High Street
Upton-upon-Severn
WR8 0HJ
tel 01684 593146
www.themapshop.co.uk

Bird-watching and nature
GOB Menorca
Molí del Rei
Camí des Castell 53
07702 Maó
tel 971-350762
www.gobmenorca.com

Centre de la Naturalesa de Menorca
Carrer Mallorca 2
Ferreries

Weather forecasts
The local newspaper, *Menorca Diario Insular*, publishes easily understood weather forecasts on its El Tiempo page.

Emergencies
If emergency assistance is required on land, phone 112 and explain the nature of the incident to an English-speaking operator. If a rescue is required, a response might be mounted by the fire service (bombers) or the police. The police can be contacted directly, either phoning 092 for the Policía Municipal, 091 for the Policía Nacional, or 062 for the Guardia Civil. Alternatively, for a medical emergency, phone 061. For sea rescues, phone 112 or 900-202202.

NOTES

LISTING OF CICERONE GUIDES

The Southern Fells
The Western Fells
Roads and Tracks of the
  Lake District
Rocky Rambler's Wild Walks
Scrambles in the Lake District
  North & South
Short Walks in Lakeland
  1 South Lakeland
  2 North Lakeland
  3 West Lakeland
The Cumbria Coastal Way
The Cumbria Way and the
  Allerdale Ramble
Tour of the Lake District

DERBYSHIRE, PEAK DISTRICT AND MIDLANDS
High Peak Walks
Scrambles in the Dark Peak
The Star Family Walks
Walking in Derbyshire
White Peak Walks
  The Northern Dales
  The Southern Dales

SOUTHERN ENGLAND
Suffolk Coast & Heaths Walks
The Cotswold Way
The North Downs Way
The Peddars Way and Norfolk
  Coast Path
The Ridgeway National Trail
The South Downs Way
The South West Coast Path
The Thames Path
Walking in Berkshire
Walking in Kent
Walking in Sussex
Walking in the Isles of Scilly
Walking in the New Forest
Walking in the Thames Valley
Walking on Dartmoor
Walking on Guernsey
Walking on Jersey
Walking on the Isle of Wight
Walks in the South Downs
  National Park

WALES AND WELSH BORDERS
Backpacker's Britain – Wales
Glyndwr's Way
Great Mountain Days
  in Snowdonia
Hillwalking in Snowdonia

Hillwalking in Wales
  Vols 1 & 2
Offa's Dyke Path
Ridges of Snowdonia
Scrambles in Snowdonia
The Ascent of Snowdon
Lleyn Peninsula Coastal Path
Pembrokeshire Coastal Path
The Shropshire Hills
The Wye Valley Walk
Walking in Pembrokeshire
Walking in the Forest of Dean
Walking in the South
  Wales Valleys
Walking on Gower
Walking on the Brecon Beacons
Welsh Winter Climbs

INTERNATIONAL CHALLENGES, COLLECTIONS AND ACTIVITIES
Canyoning
Europe's High Points
The Via Francigena
  (Canterbury to Rome): Part 1

EUROPEAN CYCLING
Cycle Touring in France
Cycle Touring in Ireland
Cycle Touring in Spain
Cycle Touring in Switzerland
Cycling in the French Alps
Cycling the Canal du Midi
Cycling the River Loire
The Danube Cycleway
The Grand Traverse of the
  Massif Central
The Rhine Cycle Route
The Way of St James

AFRICA
Climbing in the Moroccan
  Anti-Atlas
Kilimanjaro
Mountaineering in the
  Moroccan High Atlas
The High Atlas
Trekking in the Atlas Mountains
Walking in the Drakensberg

ALPS – CROSS-BORDER ROUTES
100 Hut Walks in the Alps
Across the Eastern Alps: E5
Alpine Points of View
Alpine Ski Mountaineering

  1 Western Alps
  2 Central and Eastern Alps
Chamonix to Zermatt
Snowshoeing
Tour of Mont Blanc
Tour of Monte Rosa
Tour of the Matterhorn
Trekking in the Alps
Walking in the Alps
Walks and Treks in the
  Maritime Alps

PYRENEES AND FRANCE/ SPAIN CROSS-BORDER ROUTES
Rock Climbs in The Pyrenees
The GR10 Trail
The Mountains of Andorra
The Pyrenean Haute Route
The Pyrenees
The Way of St James
  France & Spain
Through the Spanish Pyrenees:
  GR11
Walks and Climbs in
  the Pyrenees

AUSTRIA
The Adlerweg
Trekking in Austria's
  Hohe Tauern
Trekking in the Stubai Alps
Trekking in the Zillertal Alps
Walking in Austria

EASTERN EUROPE
The High Tatras
The Mountains of Romania
Walking in Bulgaria's
  National Parks
Walking in Hungary

FRANCE
Chamonix Mountain Adventures
Ecrins National Park
GR20: Corsica
Mont Blanc Walks
Mountain Adventures in
  the Maurienne
The Cathar Way
The GR5 Trail
The Robert Louis Stevenson Trail
Tour of the Oisans: The GR54
Tour of the Queyras
Tour of the Vanoise
Trekking in the Vosges and Jura

Vanoise Ski Touring
Walking in the Auvergne
Walking in the Cathar Region
Walking in the Cevennes
Walking in the Dordogne
Walking in the Haute Savoie
    North & South
Walking in the Languedoc
Walking in the Tarentaise and
    Beaufortain Alps
Walking on Corsica

GERMANY
Germany's Romantic Road
Walking in the Bavarian Alps
Walking the River Rhine Trail

HIMALAYA
8000m
Annapurna
Bhutan
Everest: A Trekker's Guide
Garhwal and Kumaon:
    A Trekker's and
    Visitor's Guide
Kangchenjunga:
    A Trekker's Guide
Langtang with Gosainkund
    and Helambu:
    A Trekker's Guide
Manaslu: A Trekker's Guide
The Mount Kailash Trek
Trekking in Ladakh
Trekking in the Himalaya

ICELAND & GREENLAND
Trekking in Greenland
Walking and Trekking in Iceland

IRELAND
Irish Coastal Walks
The Irish Coast to Coast Walk
The Mountains of Ireland

ITALY
Gran Paradiso
Sibillini National Park
Stelvio National Park
Shorter Walks in the Dolomites
Through the Italian Alps
Trekking in the Apennines
Trekking in the Dolomites
Via Ferratas of the Italian
    Dolomites: Vols 1 & 2
Walking in Abruzzo
Walking in Sardinia

Walking in Sicily
Walking in the Central
    Italian Alps
Walking in the Dolomites
Walking in Tuscany
Walking on the Amalfi Coast
Walking the Italian Lakes

MEDITERRANEAN
Jordan – Walks, Treks, Caves,
    Climbs and Canyons
The Ala Dag
The High Mountains of Crete
The Mountains of Greece
Treks and Climbs in Wadi Rum,
    Jordan
Walking in Malta
Western Crete

NORTH AMERICA
British Columbia
The Grand Canyon
The John Muir Trail
The Pacific Crest Trail

SOUTH AMERICA
Aconcagua and the
    Southern Andes
Hiking and Biking Peru's
    Inca Trails
Torres del Paine

SCANDINAVIA
Walking in Norway

SLOVENIA, CROATIA AND
MONTENEGRO
The Julian Alps of Slovenia
The Mountains of Montenegro
Trekking in Slovenia
Walking in Croatia
Walking in Slovenia:
    The Karavanke

SPAIN AND PORTUGAL
Costa Blanca: West
Mountain Walking in
    Southern Catalunya
The Mountains of Central Spain
The Northern Caminos
Trekking through Mallorca
Walking in Madeira
Walking in Mallorca
Walking in the Algarve
Walking in the Cordillera
    Cantabrica
Walking in the Sierra Nevada

Walking on Gran Canaria
Walking on La Gomera and
    El Hierro
Walking on La Palma
Walking on Tenerife
Walking the GR7 in Andalucia
Walks and Climbs in the
    Picos de Europa

SWITZERLAND
Alpine Pass Route
Canyoning in the Alps
Central Switzerland
The Bernese Alps
The Swiss Alps
Tour of the Jungfrau Region
Walking in the Valais
Walking in Ticino
Walks in the Engadine

TECHNIQUES
Geocaching in the UK
Indoor Climbing
Lightweight Camping
Map and Compass
Mountain Weather
Outdoor Photography
Polar Exploration
Rock Climbing
Sport Climbing
The Book of the Bivvy
The Hillwalker's Guide to
    Mountaineering
The Hillwalker's Manual

MINI GUIDES
Avalanche!
Navigating with a GPS
Navigation
Pocket First Aid and
    Wilderness Medicine
Snow

For full information on all
our guides, and to order
books and eBooks, visit our
website:
www.cicerone.co.uk.

Walking – Trekking – Mountaineering – Climbing – Cycling

Over 40 years, Cicerone have built up an outstanding collection of 300 guides, inspiring all sorts of amazing adventures.

Every guide comes from extensive exploration and research by our expert authors, all with a passion for their subjects. They are frequently praised, endorsed and used by clubs, instructors and outdoor organisations.

All our titles can now be bought as **e-books** and many as iPad and Kindle files and we will continue to make all our guides available for these and many other devices.

Our website shows any **new information** we've received since a book was published. Please do let us know if you find anything has changed, so that we can pass on the latest details. On our **website** you'll also find some great ideas and lots of information, including sample chapters, contents lists, reviews, articles and a photo gallery.

It's easy to keep in touch with what's going on at Cicerone, by getting our monthly **free e-newsletter**, which is full of offers, competitions, up-to-date information and topical articles. You can subscribe on our home page and also follow us on **Facebook** and **Twitter**, as well as our **blog**.

Cicerone – the very best guides for exploring the world.

CICERONE

2 Police Square Milnthorpe Cumbria LA7 7PY
Tel: 015395 62069 info@cicerone.co.uk
www.cicerone.co.uk